2nd Edition

Cloud Computing

Simply In Depth

Ajit Singh

ACKNOWLEDGEMENT

This piece of study of **Cloud Computing** is an outcome of the encouragement, guidance, help and assistance provided to me by our colleagues, Sr. faculties, Tech-friends and our family members.

As an aknowledgement, I would like to take the opportunity to express our deep sense of gratitude to all those who played a crucial role in the successful completion of this book, especially to our sr. students; this book certainly has been benefited from discussions held with many IT professionals (Ex-students) over the years it took me to write it.

My primary goal here is to provide a sufficient introduction and details of the **Cloud Computing** so that the students can have an efficient knowledge about **Cloud Computing**. Moreover, it presupposes knowledge of the principles and concepts of the Internet & Business over Internet. On the same note, any errors and inaccuracies are our responsibility and any suggestions in this regard are warmly welcomed!

Finally, I would like to thank the **Kindle Direct Publishing** team and **Amazon** team for its enthusiastic online support and guidance in bringing out this book.

I hope that the reader will like this book and find it useful in learning the concepts of **Cloud Computing** with practical implementation of Amazon's AWS..

Thank You !!

Ajit Singh

PREFACE

Share the knowledge,

Strenghten the surrounding......!!

The study/learning of **Cloud Computing** is an essential part of any computer science education and of course for the B.Tech / MCA / M.Tech courses of several Universities across the world, including AICTE compatible syllabus. This textbook is intended as a guide for an explanatory course of **Cloud Computing** for the Graduate and Post Graduate Students of several universities across the world.

Cloud Computing has recently emerged as one of the buzzwords of ICT industry. Numerous IT vendors are promising to offer computation, storage and application hosting services and to provide coverage in several continents, offering service-level agreements backed performance and uptime promises for their services. While these 'clouds' are the natural evolution of traditional data centers, they are distinguished by exposing resources as standards-based Web services and following a 'utility' pricing model where customers are charged based on their utilization of computational resources.

Cloud computing is considered the evolution of a variety of technologies that have come together to change an organizations' approach for building their IT infrastructure. Actually, there is nothing new in any of the technologies that are used in the cloud computing where most of these technologies have been known for ages. It is all about making them all accessible to the masses under the name of cloud computing. Cloud is not simply the latest term for the Internet, though the Internet is a necessary foundation for the cloud, the cloud is something more than the Internet. The cloud is where you go to use technology when you need it, for as long as you need it. You do not install anything on your desktop, and you do not pay for the technology when you are not using it.

To The Student

This book is an introduction to the complex and emerging world of the **Cloud Computing**. It helps you understand the principles and acquire the practical skills of Amazons's AWS. This book is an introduction to the emerging world of the Cloud Computing. It helps you understand the principles, implementation, operation & security of Cloud Computing. My aim is for you to gain sufficient knowledge and experience with Cloud Computing using the best up-to-date techniques. I have tried for it to be the easiest book from which you can learn the Cloud Computing.

I have chosen the topics for this book to cover what is needed to get started with Cloud Computing, not just what is easy to teach and learn. On the other hand, I won't waste your time with material of marginal practical importance. If an idea is explained here, it's because you'll almost certainly need it.

This book is emphatically focused on "the concept". Understanding the fundamental ideas, principles, and techniques is the essence of a good implementation of cloud computing. Through this book, I hope that you will see the absolute necessity of understanding Cloud Computing.

Feedback

I have attempted to wash out every error in my 2nd edition of this book after being reviewed by lots of scholars of Computer Science, but as happens with Amazon's AWS – "A few bugs difficult to understand shall remain" – and therefore, suggestions from students that may lead to improvement of next edition in shortcoming future are highly appreciated.

Conclusive suggestions and criticism always go a long way in enhancing any endeavour. We request all readers to email us their valuable comments / views / feedback for the betterment of the book at ajit_singh24@yahoo.com mentioning the title and author name in the subject line. Please report any piracy spotted by you as well . I would be glad to hear suggestions from you.

I hope, you enjoy reading this book as much as we have enjoyed writing it. We would be glad to hear suggestions from you.

About the Author

Cloud Computing
2nd Edition

Library of Congress Control Number: 2021908564

Ajit Singh

Ajit can be contacted via one of two places:
    http://facebook.com/ajitseries
    http://amazon.com/author/ajitsingh

        Email: ajit_singh24@yahoo.com
        Ph: +91-92-346-11498

CONTENTS

1

Introduction

Cloud computing can be defined as a model for enabling ubiquitous, convenient and on-demand network access to a shared pool of configurable computing resources that can be rapidly provisioned and released with minimal management effort from the user side and minimal service provider interaction.

Cloud computing is considered the evolution of a variety of technologies that have come together to change an organizations' approach for building their IT infrastructure. Actually, there is nothing new in any of the technologies that are used in the cloud computing where most of these technologies have been known for ages. It is all about making them all accessible to the masses under the name of cloud computing. Cloud is not simply the latest term for the Internet, though the Internet is a necessary foundation for the cloud, the cloud is something more than the Internet. The cloud is where you go to use technology when you need it, for as long as you need it. You do not install anything on your desktop, and you do not pay for the technology when you are not using it.

The cloud can be both software and infrastructure. It can be an application you access through the Web or a server like Gmail and it can be also an IT infrastructure that can be used as per user's request. Whether a service is software or hardware, the following is a simple test to determine whether that service is a *cloud service*:

Cloud computing is the delivery of on-demand computing services – from applications to storage and processing power – typically over the internet and on a pay-as-you-go basis.

If you can walk into any place and sit down at any computer without preference for operating system or browser and access a service, that service is cloud-based. Generally, there are three measures used to decide whether a particular service is a cloud service or not:

➤ The service is accessible via a web browser or web services API.
➤ Zero capital expenditure is necessary to get started.
➤ You pay only for what you use.

Historical Evolution

The vision of organizing compute resources as a utility grid materialized in the 1990s as an effort to solve grand challenges in scientific computing. The technology that was developed is referred to as Grid Computing and in practice involved interconnecting high-performance computing facilities across universities in regional, national, and pan-continent Grids. Grid middle-ware was concerned with transferring huge amounts of data, executing computational tasks across administrative domains, and allocating resources shared across projects fairly. Given that you did not pay for the resources you used, but were granted them based on your project mem-bership, a lot of effort was spent on sophisticated security policy configuration and validation. The complex policy landscape that ensued hindered the uptake of Grid com-puting technology commercially. Compare this model to the pay-per-use model of Cloud computing and it then becomes easy to see what, in particular, smaller businesses preferred. Another important mantra of the Grid was that local system administrators should have the last say and full control of the allocation of their resources. No remote users should have full control or root access to the expen-sive super computer machines, but could declare what kind of software they required to run their jobs. Inherently in this architecture is the notion of batch jobs. Interactive usage or continuous usage where you installed, config-ured and ran your own software, such as a Web server was not possible on the Grid. Virtual machine technol-ogy [3] released the Cloud users from this constraint, but the fact that it was very clear who pays for the usage of a machine in the Cloud also played a big role. In summary, these restrictions stopped many of the Grid protocols from spreading beyond the scientific computing domain, and also eventually resulted in many scientific computing projects migrating to Cloud technology.

Cloud computing as a term has been around since the early 2000s, but the concept of computing-as-a-service has been around for much, much longer -- as far back as the 1960s, when computer bureaus would allow companies to rent time on a mainframe, rather than have to buy one themselves.

These 'time-sharing' services were largely overtaken by the rise of the PC which made owning a computer much more affordable, and then by the rise of corporate data centers where companies would store vast amounts of data.

But the concept of renting access to computing power has resurfaced a number of times since then -- in the application service providers, utility computing, and grid computing of the late 1990s and early 2000s. This was followed by cloud computing, which really took hold with the emergence of software as a service and hyperscale cloud computing providers such as Amazon Web Services.

NIST Cloud Computing Reference

After years in the works and 15 drafts, the **National Institute of Standards and Technology's (NIST)** working definition of cloud computing, the 16th and final definition has been published as *The NIST Definition of Cloud Computing* (NIST Special Publication 800-145).

Cloud computing is a relatively new business model in the computing world. According to the official NIST definition, "cloud computing is a model for enabling ubiquitous, convenient, on-demand network access to a shared pool of configurable computing resources (e.g., networks, servers, storage, applications and services) that can be rapidly provisioned and released with minimal management effort or service provider interaction."

The NIST definition lists five essential characteristics of cloud computing: on-demand self-service, broad network access, resource pooling, rapid elasticity or expansion, and measured service. It also lists three "service models" (software, platform and infrastructure), and four "deployment models" (private, community, public and hybrid) that together categorize ways to deliver cloud services. The definition is intended to serve as a means for broad comparisons of cloud services and deployment strategies, and to provide a baseline for discussion from what is cloud computing to how to best use cloud computing.

"When agencies or companies use this definition," says NIST computer scientist Peter Mell, "they have a tool to determine the extent to which the information technology implementations they are considering meet the cloud characteristics and models. This is important because by adopting an authentic cloud, they are more likely to reap the promised benefits of cloud—cost savings, energy savings, rapid deployment and customer empowerment. And matching an implementation to the cloud definition can assist in evaluating the security properties of the cloud."

While just finalized, NIST's working definition of cloud computing has long been the de facto definition. In fact before it was officially published, the draft was the U.S. contribution to the InterNational Committee for Information Technology Standards (INCITS) as that group worked to develop a standard international cloud computing definition.

The first draft of the cloud computing definition was created in November 2009. "We went through many versions while vetting it with government and industry before we had a stable one." That one, version 15, was posted to the NIST cloud computing website in July 2009. In January 2011 that version was published for public comment as public draft SP 800-145.

NIST Definition of Cloud Computing

A good starting point for a definition of cloud computing is the definition issued by the U.S. National Institute of Standards and Technology (NIST) September, 2011. It starts with:

Cloud computing is a model for enabling ubiquitous, convenient, on-demand network access to a shared pool of configurable computing resources (e.g., networks, servers, storage, applications, and services) that can be rapidly provisioned and released with minimal management effort or service provider interaction. This cloud model is composed of five essential characteristics, three service models, and four deployment models.

Before getting to the essential characteristics, service models, and deployment models of the cloud model mentioned at the end of the definition, let's pause for a moment and consider this first part of the first sentence. It mentions a *shared pool of configurable computing resources*. This aspect of Cloud Computing is not new. In fact, it is fair to draw a direct line from time-sharing—that was initiated in the late 1950s and saw significant growth in the 1960s and 1970s—to today's Cloud Computing. Adding to that, however, is the essential characteristic of Cloud Computing known as *elasticity*. The second part of the first sentence alludes to elasticity by stating there are *computing resources ... that can be rapidly provisioned and released with minimal management effort or service provider interaction.* (We'll get to *service provider* later.)

The end of the first sentence of the definition mentions a *service provider*. In Cloud Computing, the elastic computing resources are used to provide a service. It is unclear how rigorous we should view the term *service* in this definition. Nevertheless, Cloud Computing is very much involved with the software engineering term *service*. A service is the endpoint of a connection. Also, a service has some type of underlying computer system that supports the connection offered (in this case the elastic computing resources). See:

Web Services and Cloud Computing

Service-Oriented Architecture (SOA) and Cloud Computing

The NIST Definition of Cloud Computing lists five essential characteristics of Cloud Computing. It is reasonable to assume that missing any one of these essential characteristics means a service or computing capability cannot be considered as Cloud Computing.

1. On-demand self-service. A consumer can unilaterally provision computing capabilities, such as server time and network storage, as needed automatically without requiring human interaction with each service provider.

2. Broad network access. Capabilities are available over the network and accessed through standard mechanisms that promote use by heterogeneous thin or thick client platforms (e.g., mobile phones, tablets, laptops, and workstations).

3. Resource pooling. The provider's computing resources are pooled to serve multiple consumers using a multi-tenant model, with different physical and virtual resources dynamically assigned and reassigned according to consumer demand. There is a sense of location independence in that the customer generally has no control or knowledge over the exact location of the provided resources but may be able to specify location at a higher level of abstraction (e.g., country, state, or datacenter). Examples of resources include storage, processing, memory, and network bandwidth.

4. Rapid elasticity. Capabilities can be elastically provisioned and released, in some cases automatically, to scale rapidly outward and inward commensurate with demand. To the consumer, the capabilities available for provisioning often appear to be unlimited and can be appropriated in any quantity at any time.

5. Measured service. Cloud systems automatically control and optimize resource use by leveraging a metering capability at some level of abstraction appropriate to the type of service (e.g., storage, processing, bandwidth, and active user accounts). Typically this is done on a pay-per-use or charge-per-use basis. Resource usage can be monitored, controlled, and reported, providing transparency for both the provider and consumer of the utilized service.

So, Cloud Computing is measured, on-demand, elastic computing using pooled resources, usually on the Internet.

Next, the NIST Definition of Cloud Computing list three service models:

1. Software as a Service (SaaS). The capability provided to the consumer is to use the provider's applications running on a cloud infrastructure2. The applications are accessible from various client devices through either a thin client interface, such as a web browser (e.g., web-based email), or a program interface. The consumer does not manage or control the underlying cloud infrastructure including network, servers, operating systems, storage, or even individual application capabilities, with the possible exception of limited user-specific application configuration settings.

2. Platform as a Service (PaaS). The capability provided to the consumer is to deploy onto the cloud infrastructure consumer-created or acquired applications created using programming languages, libraries, services, and tools supported by the provider. The consumer does not manage or control the underlying cloud infrastructure including network, servers, operating systems, or storage, but has control over the deployed applications and possibly configuration settings for the application-hosting environment.

3. Infrastructure as a Service (IaaS). The capability provided to the consumer is to provision processing, storage, networks, and other fundamental computing resources where the consumer is able to deploy and run arbitrary software, which can include operating systems and applications. The consumer does not manage or control the underlying cloud infrastructure but has control over operating systems, storage, and deployed applications; and possibly limited control of select networking components (e.g., host firewalls)..

Finally, the NIST Defination of Cloud Computing lists four deployment models:

Deployment Models

Deploying cloud computing can differ depending on requirements, and the following four deployment models have been identified, each with specific characteristics that support the needs of the services and users of the clouds in particular ways.

	Private Cloud
	Community Cloud
	Public Cloud
	Hybrid Cloud

Private Cloud — The cloud infrastructure has been deployed, and is maintained and operated for a specific organization.. The operation may be in-house or with a third party on the premises..

Community Cloud — The cloud infrastructure is shared among a number of organizations with similar interests and requirements.. This may help limit the capital expenditure costs for its establishment as the costs are shared among the organizations.. The operation may be in-house or with a third party on the premises..

Public Cloud — The cloud infrastructure is available to the public on a commercial basis by a cloud service provider.. This enables a consumer to develop and deploy a service in the cloud with very little financial outlay compared to the capital expenditure requirements normally associated with other deployment options..

Hybrid Cloud — The cloud infrastructure consists of a number of clouds of any type,but the clouds have the ability through their interfaces to allow data and/or applications to be moved from one cloud to another.. This can be a combination of private and public clouds that support the requirement to retain some data in an organization, and also the need to offer services in the cloud.

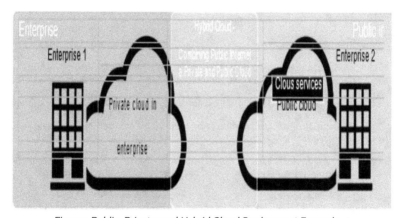

Figure: Public, Private, and Hybrid Cloud Deployment Example

Why is it called cloud computing?

A fundamental concept behind cloud computing is that the location of the service, nd many of the details such as the hardware or operating system on which it is running, are largely irrelevant to the user. It's with this in mind that the metaphor of the cloud was borrowed from old telecoms network schematics, in which the public telephone network (and later the internet) was often represented as a cloud to denote that the underlying technologies were irrelevant.

The term "Cloud" came from a network design that was used by network engineers to represent the location of various network devices and there inter-connection. The shape of this network design was like a cloud.

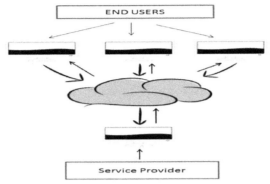

Figure: Cloud Shape

Why Cloud Computing?

With increase in computer and Mobile user's, data storage has become a priority in all fields. Large and small scale businesses today thrive on their data & they spent a huge amount of money to maintain this data. It requires a strong IT support and a storage hub. Not all businesses can afford high cost of in-house IT infrastructure and back up support services. For them Cloud Computing is a cheaper solution. Perhaps its efficiency in storing data, computation and less maintenance cost has succeeded to attract even bigger businesses as well.

Cloud computing decreases the hardware and software demand from the user's side. The only thing that user must be able to run is the cloud computing systems interface software, which can be as simple as Web browser, and the Cloud network takes care of the rest. We all have experienced cloud computing at some instant of time, some of the popular cloud services we have used or we are still using are mail services like gmail, hotmail or yahoo etc.

While accessing e-mail service our data is stored on cloud server and not on our computer. The technology and infrastructure behind the cloud is invisible. It is less important whether cloud services are based on HTTP, XML, Ruby, PHP or other specific technologies as far as it is user friendly and functional. An individual user can connect to cloud system from his/her own devices like desktop, laptop or mobile.

Cloud computing harnesses small business effectively having limited resources, it gives small businesses access to the technologies that previously were out of their reach. Cloud computing helps small businesses to convert their maintenance cost into profit. Let's see how?

In an in-house IT server, you have to pay a lot of attention and ensure that there are no flaws into the system so that it runs smoothly. And in case of any technical glitch you are completely responsible; it will seek a lot of attention, time and money for repair. Whereas, in cloud computing, the service provider takes the complete responsibility of the complication and the technical faults.

What cloud computing services are available?

Cloud computing services cover a vast range of options now, from the basics of storage, networking, and processing power through to natural language processing and artificial intelligence as well as standard office applications. Pretty much any service that doesn't require you to be physically close to the computer hardware that you are using can now be delivered via the cloud. Many companies are delivering services from the cloud.. Some notable examples include the following:

• Google — Has a private cloud that it uses for delivering Google Docs and many other services to its users, including email access, document applications, text translations, maps, web analytics, and much more..

• Microsoft — Has Microsoft® Office 365® online service that allows for content and business intelligence tools to be moved into the cloud, and Microsoft currently makes its office applications available in a cloud..

• Salesforce.com — Runs its application set for its customers in a cloud, and its Force..com and Vmforce..com products provide developers with platforms to build customized cloud services..

Cloud computing underpins a vast number of services. That includes consumer services like Gmail or the cloud back-up of the photos on your smartphone, though to the services which allow large enterprises to host all their data and run all of their applications in the cloud. Netflix relies on cloud computing services to run its video streaming service and its other business systems too, and have a number of other organizations.

Cloud computing is becoming the default option for many apps: software vendors are increasingly offering their applications as services over the internet rather than standalone products as they try to switch to a subscription model. However, there is a potential downside to cloud computing, in that it can also introduce new costs and new risks for companies using it.

How Cloud Computing Works?

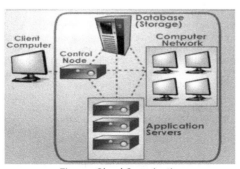

Figure: Cloud Organisation

Let's say you're an executive at a large corporation. Your particular responsibilities include making sure that all of your employees have the right hardware and software they need to do their jobs. Buying computers for everyone isn't enough -- you also have to purchase software or software licenses to give employees the tools they require. Whenever you have a new hire, you have to buy more software or make sure your current software license allows another user. It's so stressful that you find it difficult to go to sleep on your huge pile of money every night.

Soon, there may be an alternative for executives like you. Instead of installing a suite of software for each computer, you'd only have to load one application. That application would allow workers to log into a Web-based service which hosts all the programs the user would need for his or her job. Remote machines owned by another company would run everything from e-mail to word processing to complex data analysis programs. It's called cloud computing, and it could change the entire computer industry.

In a cloud computing system, there's a significant workload shift. Local computers no longer have to do all the heavy lifting when it comes to running applications. The network of computers that make up the cloud handles them instead. Hardware and software demands on the user's side decrease. The only thing the user's computer needs to be able to run is the cloud computing system's interface software, which can be as simple as a Web browser, and the cloud's network takes care of the rest.

There's a good chance you've already used some form of cloud computing. If you have an e-mail account with a Web-based e-mail service like Hotmail, Yahoo! Mail or Gmail, then you've had some experience with cloud computing. Instead of running an e-mail program on your computer, you log in to a Web e-mail account remotely. The software and storage for your account doesn't exist on your computer -- it's on the service's computer cloud.

Cloud computing region & availability zone

Cloud computing services are operated from giant datacenters around the world. AWS divides this up by 'regions' and 'availability zones'. Each AWS region is a separate geographic area, like EU (London) or US West (Oregon), which AWS then further subdivides into what it calls availability zones (AZs). An AZ is composed of one or more datacenters that are far enough apart that in theory a single disaster won't take both offline, but close enough together for business continuity applications that require rapid failover. Each AZ has multiple internet connections and power connections to multiple grids: AWS has over 50 AZs.
Google uses a similar model, dividing its cloud computing resources into regions which are then subdivided into zones, which include one or more datacenters from which customers can run their services. It currently has 15 regions made up of 44 zones: Google recommends customers deploy applications across multiple zones and regions to help protect against unexpected failures.

Microsoft Azure divides its resources slightly differently. It offers regions which it describes as is a "set of datacentres deployed within a latency-defined perimeter and connected through a dedicated regional low-latency network". It also offers 'geographies' typically containing two or more regions, that can be used by customers with specific data-residency and compliance needs "to keep their data and apps close". It also offers availability zones made up of one or more data centres equipped with independent power, cooling and networking.

Cloud computing and power usage

Those data centers are also sucking up a huge amount of power: for example Microsoft recently struck a deal with GE to buy all of the output from its new 37-megawatt wind farm in Ireland for the next 15 years in order to power its cloud data centers. Ireland said it now expects data centers to account for 15 percent of total energy demand by 2026, up from less than two percent back in 2015.

Cloud computing: IBM overhauls access rules at Euro data centre

AWS just sold some of its cloud computing infrastructure in China

How important is the cloud?

Building the infrastructure to support cloud computing now accounts for more than a third of all IT spending worldwide, according to research from IDC. Meanwhile spending on traditional, in-house IT continues to slide as computing workloads continue to move to the cloud, whether that is public cloud services offered by vendors or private clouds built by enterprises themselves.
451 Research predicts that around one-third of enterprise IT spending will be on hosting and cloud services this year "indicating a growing reliance on external sources of infrastructure, application, management and security services". Analyst Gartner predicts that half of global enterprises using the cloud now will have gone all-in on it by 2021.

According to Gartner, global spending on cloud services will reach $260bn this year up from $219.6bn. It's also growing at a faster rate than the analysts expected. But it's not entirely clear how much of that demand is coming from businesses that actually want to move to the cloud and how much is being created by vendors who now only offer cloud versions of their products (often because they are keen to move to away from selling one-off licences to selling potentially more lucrative and predictable cloud subscriptions).

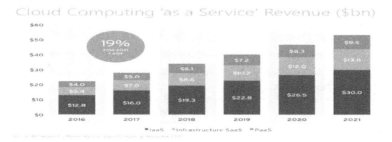

Grid Computing Vs Cloud Computing

When we switch on the fan or any electric device, we are less concern about the power supply from where it comes and how it is generated. The power supply or electricity that we receives at our home travels through a chain of network, which includes power stations, transformers, power lines and transmission stations. These components together make a 'Power Grid'. Likewise, 'Grid Computing' is an infrastructure that links computing resources such as PCs, servers, workstations and storage elements and provides the mechanism required to access them.

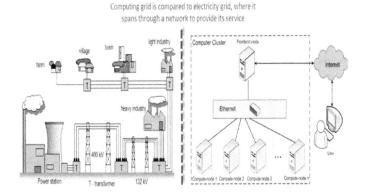

Computing grid is compared to electricity grid, where it
spans through a network to provide its service

Grid Computing is a middle ware to co-ordinate disparate IT resources across a network, allowing them to function as whole. It is more often used in scientific research and in universities for educational purpose. For example, a group of architect students working on a different project requires a specific designing tool and a software for designing purpose but only couple of them got access to this designing tool, the problem is how they can make this tool available to rest of the students. To make available for other students they will put this designing tool on campus network, now the grid will connect all these computers in campus network and allow student to use designing tool required for their project from anywhere.

Cloud computing and Grid computing is often confused, though there functions are almost similar there approach for their functionality is different. Let see how they operate-

Cloud Computing	Grid Computing
Cloud computing works more as a service provider for utilizing computer resource	Grid computing uses the available resource and interconnected computer systems to accomplish a commo

Comparison of Cloud technology with traditional computing

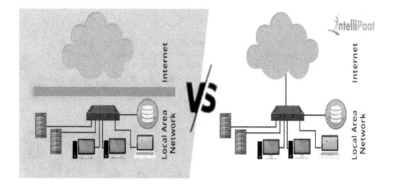

We have made an effort to show how Cloud Computing trumps over the traditional computing. You can see how the CSP is virtually taking care of all the responsibilities we have mentioned below.

Parameters	Traditional computing	Cloud Computing services
Pricing	A firm would need huge upfront cost for both hardware and software	Economical and predictable
Security	To ensure security the firm's IT experts should be better than hackers	Cloud services are regularly checked for any security fault lines
Technical support	Contractual or per instance billing of any technical glitches	Unlimited technical support which comes within the ambit of subscription fee
Infrastructure	Standalone server hardware and server software which is pricey	Multi-tenant systems shared by multiple cloud customers
Reliability	Depends on backup and in-house IT skills	Professional technical expertise included within the subscription fee
Accountability	After initial setup, provider is not typically bothered with accountability	The cloud provider can be held fully accountable for any misgivings in the cloud services

Applications of Cloud Computing

Big data analytics – Garnering valuable business value from vast amount of unstructured and structured data is all possible through Cloud Computing technology. Retailers are deriving value from customers' buying patterns. This they leverage to produce efficient marketing and advertising platforms. Social networking platforms are analyzing behavioral patterns of millions of people across the world to get meaningful information.

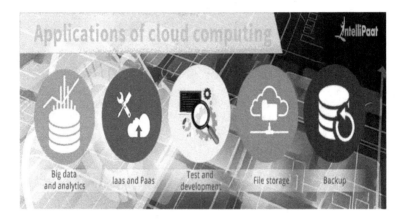

IaaS and PaaS – Instead of investing in an on-premise infrastructure, firms can instead use IaaS services on a pay-per-use model. AWS is undisputedly the leading provider of IaaS services with its IaaS cloud being 10 times bigger than its next competitors combined. PaaS is used to enhance the development cycle on a ready-to-use platform. IaaS and PaaS are among the best Cloud Computing examples.

Test and development – Doing this process is tedious. First you have to set up a budget, environment, manpower and time. Then you have to install and configure your platform. You can instead opt for cloud services where already existing environments can serve you well in this regard.

File storage – Imagine a web interface through which you can store all the data you need and expect it to be there safe and secure. That's what organizations are considering where they pay only for the amount of storage they put into the cloud. Multi tenant storage in the cloud infrastructure makes all this possible.

Backup – Traditional backup practices had problems like running out of backup media, heavy time required to load backup devices for a restore operation.

Backup in Cloud Computing technology doesn't compromise on security, availability, and capacity and it is seamless.

Benefits

The following are some of the possible benefits for those who offer cloud computing-based services and applications:

• Cost Savings – Companies can reduce their capital expenditures and use operational expenditures for increasing their computing capabilities.. This is a lower barrier to entry and also requires fewer in-house IT resources to provide system support..

• Scalability/Flexibility – Companies can start with a small deployment and grow to a large deployment fairly rapidly, and then scale back if necessary.. Also, the flexibility of cloud computing allows companies to use extra resources at peak times, enabling them to satisfy consumer demands..

• Reliability – Services using multiple redundant sites can support business continuity and disaster recovery..

• Maintenance – Cloud service providers do the system maintenance, and access is through APIs that do not require application installations onto PCs, thus further reducing maintenance requirements..

• Mobile Accessible – Mobile workers have increased productivity due to systems accessible in an infrastructure available from anywhere..

Challenges

The following are some of the notable challenges associated with cloud computing, and although some of these may cause a slowdown when delivering more services in the cloud, most also can provide opportunities, if resolved with due care and attention in the planning stages..

• Security and Privacy – Perhaps two of the more "hot button" issues surrounding cloud computing relate to storing and securing data, and monitoring the use of the cloud by the service providers.. These issues are generally attributed to slowing the deployment of cloud services.. These challenges can be addressed, for example, by storing the information internal to the organization, but allowing it to be used in the cloud.. For this to occur, though, the security mechanisms between organization and the cloud need to be robust and a Hybrid cloud could support such a deployment..

• Lack of Standards – Clouds have documented interfaces; however, no standards are associated with these, and thus it is unlikely that most clouds will be interoperable.. The Open Grid Forum is developing an Open Cloud Computing Interface to resolve this issue and the Open Cloud Consortium is working on cloud computing standards and practices.. The findings of these groups will need to mature, but it is not known whether they will address the needs of the people deploying the services and the specific interfaces these services need..

However, keeping up to date on the latest standards as they evolve will allow them to be leveraged, if applicable..

• Continuously Evolving – User requirements are continuously evolving, as are the requirements for interfaces, networking, and storage.. This means that a "cloud," especially a public one, does not remain static and is also continuously evolving..

• Compliance Concerns – The Sarbanes-Oxley Act (SOX) in the US and Data Protection directives in the EU are just two among many compliance issues affecting cloud computing, based on the type of data and application for which the cloud is being used.. The EU has a legislative backing for data protection across all member states, but in the US data protection is different and can vary from state to state.. As with security and privacy mentioned previously, these typically result in Hybrid cloud deployment with one cloud storing the data internal to the organization..

2
Cloud Enabling Technologies

Service-oriented architecture (SOA) is a software development model for distributed application components that incorporates discovery, access control, data mapping and security features.

SOA has two major functions. The first is to create a broad architectural model that defines the goals of applications and the approaches that will help meet those goals. The second function is to define specific implementation specifications, usually linked to the formal Web Services Description Language (WSDL) and Simple Object Access Protocol (SOAP) specifications.

The emergence of SOA

For decades, software development required the use of modular functional elements that perform a specific job in multiple places within an application. As application integration and component-sharing operations became linked to pools of hosting resources and distributed databases, enterprises needed a way to adapt their procedure-based development model to the use of remote, distributed components. Simple models like the remote procedure call (RPC) were a start in the right direction, but RPC lacked the security and data-independent features needed for truly open and distributed operations.

The solution to this problem was to redefine the old operation model into a broader and more clearly architected collection of services that could be provided to an application using fully distributed software components. The architecture that wrapped these services in mechanisms to support open use under full security and governance was called the service-oriented architecture, or SOA. SOA was introduced in the late 1990s as a set of principles or requirements; within a decade, there were several suitable implementations.

Major objectives of SOA

There are three major objectives of SOA, all which focus on a different part of the application lifecycle.

The first objective aims to structure procedures or software components as services. These services are designed to be loosely coupled to applications, so they are only used when needed. They are also designed to be easily utilized by software developers, who have to create applications in a consistent way.

The second objective is to provide a mechanism for publishing available services, which includes their functionality and input/output (I/O) requirements. Services are published in a way that allows developers to easily incorporate them into applications.

The third objective of SOA is to control the use of these services to avoid security and governance problems. Security in SOA revolves heavily around the security of the individual components within the architecture, identity and authentication procedures related to those components, and securing the actual connections between the components of the architecture.

WS and WSDL models

Initially, SOA implementations were based on the RPC and object-broker technologies available around 2000. But SOA quickly split into two camps. The first is the web services (WS) camp, which represents highly architected and formalized management of remote procedures and components. The second is the representational state transfer (REST) camp, which represents the use of internet technology to access remotely hosted components of applications.

The WS model of SOA uses the WSDL to connect interfaces with services and the SOAP to define procedure or component APIs. WS principles were used to link applications via an enterprise service bus (ESB), which helped businesses integrate their applications, ensure efficiency and improve data governance.

A whole series of WS standards were developed and promoted by industry giants, such as IBM and Microsoft. These standards offered a secure and flexible way to divide software into a series of distributed pieces. However, the model was difficult to use and often introduced considerable overhead into the workflows that passed between components of an application.

The WS model of SOA never reached the adoption levels that advocates had predicted; in fact, it collided with another model of remote components based on the internet: REST. RESTful application program interfaces (APIs) offered low overhead and were easy to understand. As the internet integrated more with applications, RESTful APIs were seen as the future.

SOA and microservices

The tension between SOA as a set of principles and SOA as a specific software implementation came to a head in the face of virtualization and cloud computing. The combination of virtualization and cloud encourages software developers to build applications from smaller functional components. Microservices, one of the critical current software trends, was the culmination of that development model. Because more components mean more interfaces and more complicated software design, the trend exposed the complexity and performance faults of most SOA implementations.

Microservice-based software architectures are actually just modernized implementations of the SOA model. The software components are developed as services to be exposed via APIs, as SOA would require. An API broker mediates access to components and ensures security and governance practices are followed. It also ensures there are software techniques to match diverse I/O formats of microservices to the applications that use them.

But SOA is as valid today as it was when first considered. SOA principles have taken us to the cloud and are supporting the most advanced cloud software development techniques in use today.

REST (REpresentational State Transfer)

REST (REpresentational State Transfer) is an architectural style for developing web services. REST is popular due to its simplicity and the fact that it builds upon existing systems and features of the internet's HTTP in order to achieve its objectives, as opposed to creating new standards, frameworks and technologies.

History of REST

REST was first coined by computer scientist Roy Fielding in his year-2000 Ph.D. dissertation at the University of California, titled *Architectural Styles and the Design of Network-based Software Architectures*.

"Representational State Transfer (REST)," described Fielding's beliefs about how best to architect distributed hypermedia systems. Fielding noted a number of boundary conditions that describe how REST-based systems should behave. These conditions are referred to as REST constraints, with four of the key constraints described below:

Use of a uniform interface (UI). As stated earlier, resources in REST-based systems should be uniquely identifiable through a single URL, and only by using the underlying methods of the network protocol, such as DELETE, PUT and GET with HTTP, should it be possible to manipulate a resource.

Client-server-based. In a REST-based system, there should be a clear delineation between the client and the server. UI and request-generating concerns are the domain of the client. Meanwhile, data access, workload management and security are the domain of the server. This separation allows loose coupling between the client and the server, and each can be developed and enhanced independent of the other.

Stateless operations. All client-server operations should be stateless, and any state management that is required should happen on the client, not the server.

RESTful resource caching. The ability to cache resources between client invocations is a priority in order to reduce latency and improve performance. As a result, all resources should allow caching unless an explicit indication is made that it is not possible.

REST URIs and URLs

Most people are familiar with the way URLs and URIs work on the web. A RESTful approach to developing applications asserts that requesting information about a resource should be as simple as invoking its URL.
For example, if a client wanted to invoke a web service that listed all of the quizzes available here at TechTarget, the URL to the web service would look something like this:
www.techtarget.com/restfulapi/**quizzes**
When invoked, the web service might respond with the following JSON string listing all of the available quizzes, one of which is about DevOps:
{ "quizzes" : ["Java", "DevOps", "IoT"] }
To get the DevOps quiz, the web service might be called using the following URL:
www.techtarget.com/restfulapi/**quizzes/DevOps**

Invoking this URL would return a JSON string listing all of the questions in the DevOps quiz. To get an individual question from the quiz, the number of the question would be added to the URL. So, to get the third question in the DevOps

quiz, the following RESTful URL would be used:
www.techtarget.com/restfulapi/**quizzes/DevOps/3**

Invoking that URL might return a JSON string such as the following:
{ "Question" : {"query":"What is your DevOps role?", "optionA":"Dev", "optionB":"Ops"} }
As you can see, the REST URLs in this example are structured in a logical and
meaningful way that identifies the exact resource being requested.

JSON and XML REST data formats

The example above shows JSON used as the data exchange format for the
RESTful interaction. The two most common data exchange formats are JSON
and XML, and many RESTful web services can use both formats interchangeably,
as long as the client can request the interaction to happen in either XML or JSON.
Note that while JSON and XML are popular data exchange formats, REST itself
does not put any restrictions on what the format should be. In fact, some RESTful
web services underline exchange binary data for the sake of efficiency. This is another
benefit to working with REST-based web services, as the software architect is
given a great deal of freedom in terms of how best to implement a service.

REST and the HTTP methods

The example above only dealt with accessing data.
The default operation of HTTP is GET, which is intended to be used when getting
data from the server. However, HTTP defines a number of other methods,
including PUT, POST and DELETE.
The REST philosophy asserts that to delete something on the server, you would
simply use the URL for the resource and specify the DELETE method of HTTP.
For saving data to the server, a URL and the PUT method would be used. For
operations that are more involved than simply saving, reading or deleting
information, the POST method of HTTP can be used.

Alternatives to REST

Alternate technologies for creating SOA-based systems or creating APIs for
invoking remote microservices include XML over HTTP (XML-RPC), CORBA, RMI
over IIOP and the Simple Object Access Protocol (SOAP).
Each technology has its own set of benefits and drawbacks, but the compelling
feature of REST that sets it apart is the fact that, rather than asking a developer
to work with a set of custom protocols or to create a special data format for
exchanging messages between a client and a server, REST insists the best way
to implement a network-based web service is to simply use the basic construct
of the network protocol itself, which in the case of the internet is HTTP.
This is an important point, as REST is not intended to apply just to the internet;
rather, its principles are intended to apply to all protocols,
including WEBDAV, FTP and so on.

REST vs. SOAP

The two competing styles for implementing web services are REST
and SOAP. The fundamental difference between the two is the philosophical

approach the two have to remotely invocations.

REST takes a resource-based approach to web-based interactions. With REST, you locate a resource on the server, and you choose to either update that resource, delete it or get some information about it.
With SOAP, the client doesn't choose to interact directly with a resource, but instead calls a service, and that service mitigates access to the various objects and resources behind the scenes.
SOAP has also built a large number of frameworks and APIs on top of HTTP, including the Web Services Description Language (WSDL), which defines the structure of data that gets passed back and forth between the client and the server.

Some problem domains are served well by the ability to stringently define the message format, or can benefit from using various SOAP-related APIs, such as WS-Eventing, WS-Notification and WS-Security. There are times when HTTP cannot provide the level of functionality an application might require, and in these cases, using SOAP is preferable.

Advantages of REST

A primary benefit of using REST, both from a client and server's perspective, is REST-based interactions happen using constructs that are familiar to anyone who is accustomed to using the internet's Hypertext Transfer Protocol (HTTP).
An example of this arrangement is REST-based interactions all communicate their status using standard HTTP status codes. So, a 404 means a requested resource wasn't found; a 401 code means the request wasn't authorized; a 200 code means everything is OK; and a 500 means there was an unrecoverable application error on the server.
Similarly, details such as encryption and data transport integrity are solved not by adding new frameworks or technologies, but instead by relying on well-known Secure Sockets Layer (SSL)encryption and Transport Layer Security (TLS). So, the entire REST architecture is built upon concepts with which most developers are already familiar.
REST is also a language-independent architectural style. REST-based applications can be written using any language, be it Java, Kotlin, .NET, AngularJS or JavaScript. As long as a programming language can make web-based requests using HTTP, it is possible for that language to be used to invoke a RESTful API or web service. Similarly, RESTful web services can be written using any language, so developers tasked with implementing such services can choose technologies that work best for their situation.
The other benefit of using REST is its pervasiveness. On the server side, there are a variety of REST-based frameworks for helping developers create RESTful web services, including RESTlet and Apache CXF. From the client side, all of the new JavaScript frameworks, such as JQuery, Node.js, Angular and EmberJS, all have standard libraries built into their APIs that make invoking RESTful web services and consuming the XML- or JSON-based data they return a relatively straightforward endeavor.

Disadvantages of REST

The benefit of REST using HTTP constructs also creates restrictions, however.

Many of the limitations of HTTP likewise turn into shortcomings of the REST architectural style. For example, HTTP does not store state-based information between request-response cycles, which means REST-based applications must be stateless and any state management tasks must be performed by the client. Similarly, since HTTP doesn't have any mechanism to send push notifications from the server to the client, it is difficult to implement any type of services where the server updates the client without the use of client-side polling of the server or some other type of web hook.

From an implementation standpoint, a common problem with REST is the fact that developers disagree with exactly what it means to be REST-based. Some software developers incorrectly consider anything that isn't SOAP-based to be RESTful. Driving this common misconception about REST is the fact that it is an architectural style, so there is no reference implementation or definitive standard that will confirm whether a given design is RESTful. As a result, there is discourse as to whether a given API conforms to REST-based principles.

Publish/Subscribe Model

Publish-subscribe (pub/sub) is a messaging pattern where publishers push messages to subscribers. In software architecture, pub/sub messaging provides instant event notifications for distributed applications, especially those that are decoupled into smaller, independent building blocks. In laymen's terms, pub/sub describes how two different parts of a messaging pattern connect and communicate with each other.

How Pub/Sub Works

Publish/ Subscribe Pattern

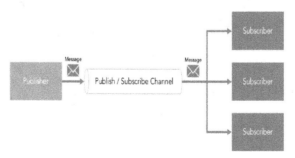

Figure – An example of a publish/subscribe messaging pattern

These are three central components to understanding pub/sub messaging pattern:
1. **Publisher:** Publishes messages to the communication infrastructure
2. **Subscriber:** Subscribes to a category of messages
3. **Communication infrastructure (channel, classes):** Receives messages from publishers and maintains subscribers' subscriptions.

The publisher will categorize published messages into classes where subscribers will then receive the message. Figure offers an illustration of this messaging pattern. Basically, a publisher has one input channel that splits into multiple output channels, one for each subscriber. Subscribers can express interest in one or more classes and only receive messages that are of interest.

The thing that makes pub/sub interesting is that the publisher and subscriber are unaware of each other. The publisher sends messages to subscribers, without knowing if there are any actually there. And the subscriber receives messages, without explicit knowledge of the publishers out there. If there are no subscribers around to receive the topic-based information, the message is dropped.

Topic and Content-Based Pub-Sub Models

In the publish–subscribe model, filtering is used to process the selection of messages for reception and processing, with the two most common being topic-based and content-based.

In a topic-based system, messages are published to named channels (topics). The publisher is the one who creates these channels. Subscribers subscribe to those topics and will receive messages from them whenever they appear.
In a content-based system, messages are only delivered if they match the constraints and criteria that are defined by the subscriber.

Example

You can check out Amazon's SNS for a simple example of a pub-sub pattern. They provide a simple notification service (SNS) that is managed by pub/sub messaging and mobile notifications service for coordinating the delivery of messages to subscribers. In other words, SNS allows you to push messages to a large amount of subscribers, distributed systems, services, and mobile devices. This makes it easy to push notifications (updates, promos, news) to iOS, Android, Fire OS, Windows and Baidu-based devices.

What are the benefits of pub/sub?

1. Loose coupling: Publishers do not know the identities of the subscribers or the message types.
2. Improved security: The communication infrastructure only publishes messages to the subscribed topics.
3. Improved testability: Topics reduce the number of messages required for testing.

Cloud Service model

The service models are categorized into three basic models:

1) Software-as-a-Service (SaaS)

2) Platform-as-a-Service (PaaS)

3) Infrastructure-as-a-Service (IaaS)

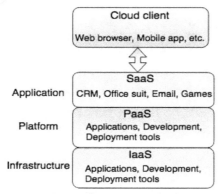

Fig. - Categories of Cloud Computing

1) Software-as-a-Service (SaaS)

SaaS is known as 'On-Demand Software'.

It is a software distribution model. In this model, the applications are hosted by a cloud service provider and publicized to the customers over internet.

In SaaS, associated data and software are hosted centrally on the cloud server.

User can access SaaS by using a thin client through a web browser.

CRM, Office Suite, Email, games, etc. are the software applications which are provided as a service through Internet.

The companies like Google, Microsoft provide their applications as a service to the end users.

Advantages of SaaS

SaaS is easy to buy because the pricing of SaaS is based on monthly or annual fee and it allows the organizations to access business functionalities at a small cost, which is less than licensed applications.

SaaS needed less hardware, because the software is hosted remotely, hence organizations do not need to invest in additional hardware.

Less maintenance cost is required for SaaS and do not require special software or hardware versions.

Disadvantages of SaaS

SaaS applications are totally dependent on Internet connection. They are not usable without Internet connection.

It is difficult to switch amongst the SaaS vendors.

2) Platform-as-a-Service (PaaS)

PaaS is a programming platform for developers. This platform is generated for the programmers to create, test, run and manage the applications.

A developer can easily write the application and deploy it directly into PaaS layer.

PaaS gives the runtime environment for application development and deployment tools.

Google Apps Engine(GAE), Windows Azure, SalesForce.com are the examples of PaaS.

Advantages of PaaS

PaaS is easier to develop. Developer can concentrate on the development and innovation without worrying about the infrastructure.

In PaaS, developer only requires a PC and an Internet connection to start building applications.

Disadvantages of PaaS

One developer can write the applications as per the platform provided by PaaS vendor hence the moving the application to another PaaS vendor is a problem.

3) Infrastructure-as-a-Service (IaaS)

IaaS is a way to deliver a cloud computing infrastructure like server, storage, network and operating system.

The customers can access these resources over cloud computing platform i.e Internet as an on-demand service.

In IaaS, you buy complete resources rather than purchasing server, software, datacenter space or network equipment.

IaaS was earlier called as Hardware as a Service(HaaS). It is a Cloud computing platform based model.

HaaS differs from IaaS in the way that users have the bare hardware on which they can deploy their own infrastructure using most appropriate software.

Advantages of IaaS

In IaaS, user can dynamically choose a CPU, memory storage configuration according to need.

Users can easily access the vast computing power available on IaaS Cloud platform.

Disadvantages of IaaS

IaaS cloud computing platform model is dependent on availability of Internet and virtualization services

How Cloud Computing Works?

The cloud has to be divided into different layers. These layers are the front-end and back-end layers. The Front-end layer is that part of the cloud with which users can interact with. For example, when we log in to our Gmail account, we see the UI (user interface) where everything works on event-driven buttons and graphics. Similarly, the software also runs in the front end of the cloud. Again, the back-end comprises hardware as well as software that delivers the back-end data from the database to the front end.

Cloud uses a network layer to connect different devices to provide access to resources residing in the centralized data center of the cloud. Cloud technology users can use the data center through the company's network or internet facilities. This technology provides various advantages; users can access the cloud from anywhere at any time, but the network bandwidth should have to be more. This technology not only facilitates desktop and laptop users, but mobile users can also access their business systems based on their demand.

As we already know that cloud computing is fast and efficient, applications running on the cloud take advantage of flexibility and computing power, i.e., the speed of processing a task. Many computers of a single organization work together along with their application on the cloud as if all the applications were running on a single machine. This flexibility of accessing the cloud resources allows users to use much or little of the resource based on the demand.

In the Cloud computing system architecture, there is another mechanism of shifting the workload. Local machines don't have to perform massive lifting operations when it comes to run applications. Cloud technology can handle those heavy loaded tasks automatically, easily, and efficiently. This brings down the hardware & software demands. The only thing that the users have to think of is the system's cloud computing interface software, which works merely as a web-browser at the front end of the user. The cloud's network takes care of the rest along with the back-end.

The back-end is connected through a virtual network or internet. Other than that, there are few more components such as Middleware, cloud resources, etc. that include cloud computing architecture. The backend is used by service providers that include various servers, computers, virtual machines & data storage facilities combined to form the cloud technology. Its dedicated server handles each application in the system. The front end includes the cloud computing system or network used to access the cloud computing system. The cloud computing systems' interface varies from cloud to cloud.

The back-end has two principal responsibilities:

- Provides traffic control mechanisms, security postures & governing the protocols.
- To employ those internet protocols that are connected to the networked computer for communication.

One central server is used to manage the entire cloud system architecture. The server is solely responsible for handling the smoothness of traffic without disruption. Middleware is a particular type of software that is used to perform processes & also connects networked computers. Depending on the client/user's demand, the storage is provided by the cloud technology's service provider.

Virtualization

The main enabling technology for Cloud Computing is Virtualization. Virtualization is a partitioning of single physical server into multiple logical servers. Once the physical server is divided, each logical server behaves like a physical server and can run an operating system and applications independently. Many popular companies's like VmWare and Microsoft provide virtualization services, where instead of using your personal PC for storage and computation, you use their virtual server. They are fast, cost-effective and less time consuming.

For software developers and testers virtualization comes very handy, as it allows developer to write code that runs in many different environments and more importantly to test that code.

Need for Virtualization
Virtualization is one of the cost and energy saving technology which allows abstraction of physical hardware to provide virtual resources in the form of Virtual Machine. Through virtualization, resources of multiple physical machines are aggregated and assigned to applications dynamically on demand. Therefore, Virtualization is defined as a key technology of Cloud Computing Environment. Using virtualization, multiple OSs and multiple applications can run on a single server at the same time, thus increasing hardware flexibility and utilization.

Virtualization is mainly used for three main purposes

1) Network Virtualization

2) Server Virtualization

3) Storage Virtualization

Network Virtualization: It is a method of combining the available resources in a network by splitting up the available bandwidth into channels, each of which is independent from the others and each channel is independent of others and can be assigned to a specific server or device in real time.

Storage Virtualization: It is the pooling of physical storage from multiple network storage devices into what appears to be a single storage device that is managed from a central console. Storage virtualization is commonly used in storage area networks (SANs).

Server Virtualization: Server virtualization is the masking of server resources like processors, RAM, operating system etc, from server users. The intention of server virtualization is to increase the resource sharing and reduce the burden and complexity of computation from users.

Virtualization is the key to unlock the Cloud system, what makes virtualization so important for the cloud is that it decouples the software from the hardware. For example, PC's can use virtual memory to borrow extra memory from the hard disk. Usually hard disk has a lot more space than memory. Although virtual disks are slower than real memory, if managed properly the substitution works perfectly. Likewise, there is software which can imitate an entire computer, which means 1 computer can perform the functions equals to 20 computers.

Components of Virtualization Environment

The main aim of the virtualization is to create logical interface by abstracting the underlying infrastructure. Some of the components of virtualization environment are discussed below:

Guest- Guest represents the system component that interacts with the virtualization layer rather than with the host.

Host- Host represents the original environment where the guests are supposed to be managed.

Virtualization layer-Virtualization layer is responsible for recreating the same or different environment where the guest will operate. It mainly deals with computation, storage and network virtualization. Virtualized resources are presented in this layer.

Characteristics of Virtualization

With reference to Cloud Computing Environment, some important characteristics of virtualization are discussed below:

Consolidation
Dedicated single system for single application concept is eliminated by Virtualization. Through virtualization multiple OSs and multiple applications can run on the same server. Both old and new versions of OS are capable of deploying on the same platform without additional investment on hardware.

Development Flexibility
Application developer can run and test their applications in heterogeneous OS environments using same virtual machine. In virtualization environment, different applications are isolated from each other in their respective virtual partition.

Migration and Cloning
To dynamically balance the workload, Virtual Machines are migrated from one site to another. As a result of which, users can access updated hardware and make recovery from hardware failure. Cloned virtual machines can be easily deployed on both local and remote sites.

Stability and Security
In virtualized environment, host OSs are capable of hosting multiple guests OSs along with multiple applications. Each virtual machine is isolated from other virtual machines and not at all interfering into each other's work which helps in achieving stability and security.

Para Virtualization
Para virtualization is an important aspect of virtualization. In virtualized environment, guest OS can run on host OS with or without modification. If any modification is made to the operating systems to be familiar with Virtual

Machine Manager, then this process is called as Para virtualization.

IMPLEMENTATION LEVELS OF VIRTUALIZATION

Virtualization is a computer architecture technology by which multiple virtual machines (VMs) are multiplexed in the same hardware machine. The idea of VMs can be dated back to the 1960s. The purpose of a VM is to enhance resource sharing by many users and improve computer performance in terms of resource utilization and application flexibility. Hardware resources (CPU, memory, I/O devices, etc.) or software resources (operating system and software libraries) can be virtualized in various functional layers. This virtualization technology has been revitalized as the demand for distributed and cloud computing increased sharply in recent years.

The idea is to separate the hardware from the software to yield better system efficiency. For example, computer users gained access to much enlarged memory space when the concept of virtual memory was introduced. Similarly, virtualization techniques can be applied to enhance the use of compute engines, networks, and storage. In this chapter we will discuss VMs and their applications for building distributed systems. According to a 2009 Gartner Report, virtualization was the top strategic technology poised to change the computer industry. With sufficient storage, any computer platform can be installed in another host computer, even if they use processors with different instruction sets and run with distinct operating systems on the same hardware.

Levels of Virtualization Implementation
A traditional computer runs with a host operating system specially tailored for its hardware architecture, as shown in Figure (a). After virtualization, different user applications managed by their own operating systems (guest OS) can run on the same hardware, independent of the host OS. This is often done by adding additional software, called a virtualization layer as shown in Figure (b). This virtualization layer is known as hypervisor or virtual machine monitor(VMM). The VMs are shown in the upper boxes, where applications run with their own guest OS over the virtualized CPU, memory, and I/O resources.

The main function of the software layer for virtualization is to virtualize the physical hardware of a host machine into virtual resources to be used by the VMs, exclusively. This can be implemented at various operational levels, as we will discuss shortly. The virtualization software creates the abstraction of VMs by interposing a virtualization layer at various levels of a computer system. Common virtualization layers include the instruction set architecture (ISA)level, hardware level, operating system level, library support level, and application level.

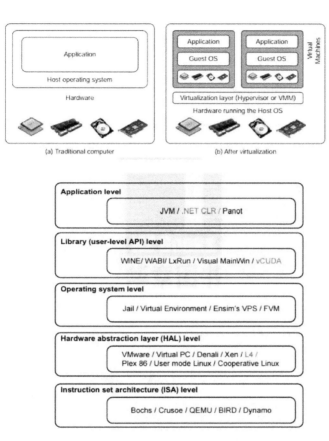

(a) Traditional computer   (b) After virtualization

| Application level |
| JVM / .NET CLR / Panot |

| Library (user-level API) level |
| WINE/ WABI/ LxRun / Visual MainWin / vCUDA |

| Operating system level |
| Jail / Virtual Environment / Ensim's VPS / FVM |

| Hardware abstraction layer (HAL) level |
| VMware / Virtual PC / Denali / Xen / L4 / Plex 86 / User mode Linux / Cooperative Linux |

| Instruction set architecture (ISA) level |
| Bochs / Crusoe / QEMU / BIRD / Dynamo |

Instruction Set Architecture Level

At the ISA level, virtualization is performed by emulating a given ISA by the ISA of the host machine. For example, MIPS binary code can run on an x86-based host machine with the help of ISA emulation. With this approach, it is possible to run a large amount of legacy binary code writ-ten for various processors on any given new hardware host machine. Instruction set emulation leads to virtual ISAs created on any hardware machine.

The basic emulation method is through code interpretation. An interpreter program interprets the source instructions to target instructions one by one. One source instruction may require tens or hundreds of native target instructions to perform its function. Obviously, this process is relatively slow. For better performance, dynamic binary translation is desired. This approach translates basic blocks of dynamic source instructions to target instructions. The basic blocks can also be extended to program traces or super blocks to increase translation efficiency. Instruction set emulation requires binary translation and optimization. A virtual instruction set architecture (V-ISA) thus requires adding a processor-specific software translation layer to the compiler.

Hardware Abstraction Level

Hardware-level virtualization is performed right on top of the bare hardware. On the one hand, this approach generates a virtual hardware environment for a VM. On the other hand, the process manages the underlying hardware through virtualization. The idea is to virtualize a computer's resources, such as its processors, memory, and I/O devices. The intention is to upgrade the hardware utilization rate by multiple users concurrently. The idea was implemented in the IBM VM/370 in the 1960s. More recently, the Xen hypervisor has been applied to virtualize x86-based machines to run Linux or other guest OS applications.

Operating System Level

This refers to an abstraction layer between traditional OS and user applications. OS-level virtualization creates isolated containers on a single physical server and the OS instances to utilize the hard-ware and software in data centers. The containers behave like real servers. OS-level virtualization is commonly used in creating virtual hosting environments to allocate hardware resources among a large number of mutually distrusting users.

Library Support Level

Most applications use APIs exported by user-level libraries rather than using lengthy system calls by the OS. Since most systems provide well-documented APIs, such an interface becomes another candidate for virtualization. Virtualization with library interfaces is possible by controlling the communication link between applications and the rest of a system through API hooks. The software tool WINE has implemented this approach to support Windows applications on top of UNIX hosts. Another example is the vCUDA which allows applications executing within VMs to leverage GPU hardware acceleration.

User-Application Level

Virtualization at the application level virtualizes an application as a VM. On a traditional OS, an application often runs as a process. Therefore, application-level virtualization is also known asprocess-level virtualization. The most popular approach is to deploy high level language (HLL)

VMs. In this scenario, the virtualization layer sits as an application program on top of the operating system, and the layer exports an abstraction of a VM that can run programs written and compiled to a particular abstract machine definition. Any program written in the HLL and compiled for this VM will be able to run on it. The Microsoft .NET CLR and Java Virtual Machine (JVM) are two good examples of this class of VM.

Other forms of application-level virtualization are known as application isolation,application sandboxing, or application streaming. The process involves wrapping the application in a layer that is isolated from the host OS and other applications. The result is an application that is much easier to distribute and remove from user workstations. An example is the LANDesk application virtualization platform which deploys software applications as self-contained, executable files in an isolated environment without requiring installation, system modifications, or elevated security privileges.

Relative Merits of Different Approaches

Table 3.1 Relative Merits of Virtualization at Various Levels (More "X"'s Means Higher Merit, with a Maximum of 5 X's)

Level of Implementation	Higher Performance	Application Flexibility	Implementation Complexity	Application Isolation
ISA	X	XXXXX	XXX	XXX
Hardware-level virtualization	XXXXX	XXX	XXXXX	XXXX
OS-level virtualization	XXXXX	XX	XXX	XX
Runtime library support	XXX	XX	XX	XX
User application level	XX	XX	XXXXX	XXXXX

VIRTUALIZATION STRUCTURES/TOOLS AND MECHANISMS

In general, there are three typical classes of VM architecture. Figure showed the architectures of a machine before and after virtualization. Before virtualization, the operating system manages the hardware. After virtualization, a virtualization layer is inserted between the hardware and the operat-ing system. In such a case, the virtualization layer is responsible for converting portions of the real hardware into virtual hardware. Therefore, different operating systems such as Linux and Windows can run on the same physical machine, simultaneously. Depending on the position of the virtualiza-tion layer, there are several classes of VM architectures, namely the hypervisor architecture, para-virtualization, and host-based virtualization. The hypervisor is also known as the VMM (Virtual Machine Monitor). They both perform the same virtualization operations.

1. Hypervisor and Xen Architecture

The hypervisor supports hardware-level virtualization on bare metal devices like CPU, memory, disk and network interfaces. The hypervisor software sits directly between the physi-cal hardware and its OS. This virtualization layer is referred to as either the VMM or the hypervisor. The hypervisor provides hypercalls for the guest OSes and applications. Depending on the functional-ity, a hypervisor can assume a micro-kernel architecture like the Microsoft Hyper-V. Or it can assume a monolithic hypervisor architecture like the VMware ESX for server virtualization.

A micro-kernel hypervisor includes only the basic and unchanging functions (such as physical memory management and processor scheduling). The device drivers and other changeable components are outside the hypervisor. A monolithic hypervisor implements all the aforementioned functions, including those of the device drivers. Therefore, the size of the hypervisor code of a micro-kernel hyper-visor is smaller than that of a monolithic hypervisor. Essentially, a hypervisor must be able to convert physical devices into virtual resources dedicated for the deployed VM to use.

The Xen Architecture

Xen is an open source hypervisor program developed by Cambridge University. Xen is a micro-kernel hypervisor, which separates the policy from the mechanism. The Xen hypervisor implements all the mechanisms, leaving the policy to be handled by Domain 0, as shown in Figure. Xen does not include any device drivers natively. It just provides a mechanism by which a guest OS can have direct access to the physical devices. As a result, the size of the Xen hypervisor is kept rather small. Xen provides a virtual environment located between the hardware and the OS. A number of vendors are in the process of developing commercial Xen hypervisors, among them are Citrix XenServer and Oracle VM.

The core components of a Xen system are the hypervisor, kernel, and applications. The organi-zation of the three components is important. Like other virtualization systems, many guest OSes can run on top of the hypervisor. However, not all guest OSes are created equal, and one in

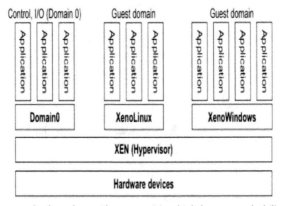

particular controls the others. The guest OS, which has control ability, is called Domain 0, and the others are called Domain U. Domain 0 is a privileged guest OS of Xen. It is first loaded when Xen boots without any file system drivers being available. Domain 0 is designed to access hardware directly and manage devices. Therefore, one of the responsibilities of Domain 0 is to allocate and map hardware resources for the guest domains (the Domain U domains).

For example, Xen is based on Linux and its security level is C2. Its management VM is named Domain 0, which has the privilege to manage other VMs implemented on the same host. If Domain 0 is compromised, the hacker can control the entire system. So, in the VM system, security policies are needed to improve the security of Domain 0. Domain 0, behaving as a VMM, allows users to create, copy, save, read, modify, share, migrate, and roll back VMs as easily as manipulating a file, which flexibly provides tremendous benefits for users.

Unfortunately, it also brings a series of security problems during the software life cycle and data lifetime.

Traditionally, a machine's lifetime can be envisioned as a straight line where the current state of the machine is a point that progresses monotonically as the software executes. During this time, con-figuration changes are made, software is installed, and patches are applied. In such an environment, the VM state is akin to a tree: At any point, execution can go into N different branches where multiple instances of a VM can exist at any point in this tree at any given time. VMs are allowed to roll back to previous states in their execution (e.g., to fix configuration errors) or rerun from the same point many times (e.g., as a means of distributing dynamic content or circulating a "live" system image).

2. Para-Virtualization Architecture

When the x86 processor is virtualized, a virtualization layer is inserted between the hardware and the OS. According to the x86 ring definition, the virtualization layer should also be installed at Ring 0. Different instructions at Ring 0 may cause some problems. In Figure 3.8, we show that para-virtualization replaces nonvirtualizable instructions with hypercalls that communicate directly with the hypervisor or VMM. However, when the guest OS kernel is modified for virtualization, it can no longer run on the hardware directly.

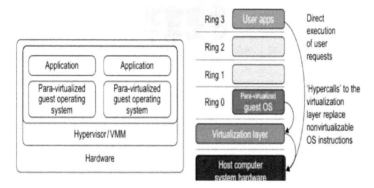

Although para-virtualization reduces the overhead, it has incurred other problems. First, its compatibility and portability may be in doubt, because it must support the unmodified OS as well. Second, the cost of maintaining para-virtualized OSes is high, because they may require deep OS kernel modifications. Finally, the performance advantage of para-virtualization varies greatly due to workload variations. Compared with full virtualization, para-virtualization is relatively easy and more practical. The main problem in full virtualization is its low performance in binary translation. To speed up binary translation is difficult. Therefore, many virtualization products employ the para-virtualization architecture. The popular Xen, KVM, and VMware ESX are good examples.

VIRTUALIZATION OF CPU, MEMORY, AND I/O DEVICES

To support virtualization, processors such as the x86 employ a special running mode and instructions, known as hardware-assisted virtualization. In this way, the VMM and guest OS run in different modes and all sensitive instructions of the guest OS and its applications are trapped in the VMM. To save processor states, mode switching is completed by hardware. For the x86 architecture, Intel and AMD have proprietary technologies for hardware-assisted virtualization.

Hardware Support for Virtualization

Modern operating systems and processors permit multiple processes to run simultaneously. If there is no protection mechanism in a processor, all instructions from different processes will access the hardware directly and cause a system crash. Therefore, all processors have at least two modes, user mode and supervisor mode, to ensure controlled access of critical hardware. Instructions running in supervisor mode are called privileged instructions. Other instructions are unprivileged instructions. In a virtualized environment, it is more difficult to make OSes and applications run correctly because there are more layers in the machine stack. Example 3.4 discusses Intel's hardware support approach.

At the time of this writing, many hardware virtualization products were available. The VMware Workstation is a VM software suite for x86 and x86-64 computers. This software suite allows users to set up multiple x86 and x86-64 virtual computers and to use one or more of these VMs simultaneously with the host operating system. The VMware Workstation assumes the host-based virtualization. Xen is a hypervisor for use in IA-32, x86-64, Itanium, and PowerPC 970 hosts. Actually, Xen modifies Linux as the lowest and most privileged layer, or a hypervisor.

One or more guest OS can run on top of the hypervisor. KVM (Kernel-based Virtual Machine) is a Linux kernel virtualization infrastructure. KVM can support hardware-assisted virtualization and paravirtualization by using the Intel VT-x or AMD-v and VirtIO framework, respectively. The VirtIO framework includes a paravirtual Ethernet card, a disk I/O controller, a balloon device for adjusting guest memory usage, and a VGA graphics interface using VMware drivers.

Example: Hardware Support for Virtualization in the Intel x86 Processor
Since software-based virtualization techniques are complicated and incur performance overhead, Intel provides a hardware-assist technique to make virtualization easy and improve performance. Figure provides an overview of Intel's full virtualization techniques. For processor virtualization, Intel offers the VT-x or VT-i technique. VT-x adds a privileged mode (VMX Root Mode) and some instructions to processors. This enhancement traps all sensitive instructions in the VMM automatically. For memory virtualization, Intel offers the EPT, which translates the virtual address to the machine's physical addresses to improve performance. For I/O virtualization, Intel implements VT-d and VT-c to support this.

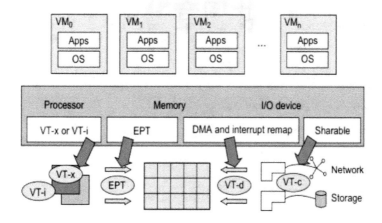

CPU Virtualization

A VM is a duplicate of an existing computer system in which a majority of the VM instructions are executed on the host processor in native mode. Thus, unprivileged instructions of VMs run directly on the host machine for higher efficiency. Other critical instructions should be handled carefully for correctness and stability. The critical instructions are divided into three categories:privileged instructions, control-sensitive instructions, and behavior-sensitive instructions. Privileged instructions execute in a privileged mode and will be trapped if executed outside this mode. Control-sensitive instructions attempt to change the configuration of resources used. Behavior-sensitive instructions have different behaviors depending on the configuration of resources, including the load and store operations over the virtual memory.

A CPU architecture is virtualizable if it supports the ability to run the VM's privileged and unprivileged instructions in the CPU's user mode while the VMM runs in supervisor mode. When the privileged instructions including control- and behavior-sensitive instructions of a VM are exe-cuted, they are trapped in the VMM. In this case, the VMM acts as a unified mediator for hardware access from different VMs to guarantee the correctness and stability of the whole system. However, not all CPU architectures are virtualizable. RISC CPU architectures can be naturally virtualized because all control- and behavior-sensitive instructions are privileged instructions. On the contrary, x86 CPU architectures are not primarily designed to support virtualization. This is because about 10 sensitive instructions, such as SGDT and SMSW, are not privileged instructions. When these instruc-tions execute in virtualization, they cannot be trapped in the VMM.

On a native UNIX-like system, a system call triggers the 80h interrupt and passes control to the OS kernel. The interrupt handler in the kernel is then invoked to process the system call. On a para-virtualization system such as Xen, a system call in the guest OS first triggers the 80hinterrupt nor-mally. Almost at the same time, the 82h interrupt in the hypervisor is triggered. Incidentally, control is passed on to the hypervisor as well. When the hypervisor completes its task for the guest OS system call, it passes control back to the guest OS kernel. Certainly, the guest OS kernel may also invoke the hypercall while it's running. Although paravirtualization of a CPU lets unmodified applications run in the VM, it causes a small performance penalty.

Hardware-Assisted CPU Virtualization

This technique attempts to simplify virtualization because full or paravirtualization is complicated. Intel and AMD add an additional mode called privilege mode level (some people call it Ring-1) to x86 processors. Therefore, operating systems can still run at Ring 0 and the hypervisor can run at Ring -1. All the privileged and sensitive instructions are trapped in the hypervisor automatically. This technique removes the difficulty of implementing binary translation of full virtualization. It also lets the operating system run in VMs without modification.

Example: Intel Hardware-Assisted CPU Virtualization
Although x86 processors are not virtualizable primarily, great effort is taken to virtualize them. They are used widely in comparing RISC processors that the bulk of x86-based legacy systems cannot discard easily. Virtuali-zation of x86 processors is detailed in the following sections. Intel's VT-x technology is an example of hardware-assisted virtualization, as shown in Figure. Intel calls the privilege level of x86 processors the VMX Root Mode. In order to control the start and stop of a VM and allocate a memory page to maintain the

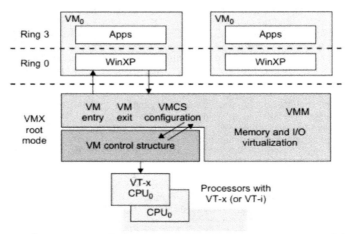

CPU state for VMs, a set of additional instructions is added. At the time of this writing, Xen, VMware, and the Microsoft Virtual PC all implement their hypervisors by using the VT-x technology.

Generally, hardware-assisted virtualization should have high efficiency. However, since the transition from the hypervisor to the guest OS incurs high overhead switches between processor modes, it sometimes cannot outperform binary translation. Hence, virtualization systems such as VMware now use a hybrid approach, in which a few tasks are offloaded to the hardware but the rest is still done in software. In addition, para-virtualization and hardware-assisted virtualization can be combined to improve the performance further.

Memory Virtualization

Virtual memory virtualization is similar to the virtual memory support provided by modern operat-ing systems. In a traditional execution environment, the operating system maintains mappings of virtual memory to machine memory using page tables, which is a one-stage mapping from virtual memory to machine memory. All modern x86 CPUs include a memory management unit (MMU) and a translation lookaside buffer (TLB) to optimize virtual memory performance. However, in a virtual execution environment, virtual memory virtualization involves sharing the physical system memory in RAM and dynamically allocating it to the physical memory of the VMs.

That means a two-stage mapping process should be maintained by the guest OS and the VMM, respectively: virtual memory to physical memory and physical memory to machine memory. Furthermore, MMU virtualization should be supported, which is transparent to the guest OS. The guest OS continues to control the mapping of virtual addresses to the physical memory addresses of VMs. But the guest OS cannot directly access the actual machine memory. The VMM is responsible for mapping the guest physical memory to the actual machine memory. Figure 3.12 shows the two-level memory mapping procedure.

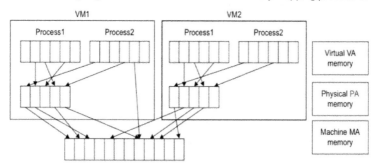

Since each page table of the guest OSes has a separate page table in the VMM corresponding to it, the VMM page table is called the shadow page table. Nested page tables add another layer of indirection to virtual memory. The MMU already handles virtual-to-physical translations as defined by the OS. Then the physical memory addresses are translated to machine addresses using another set of page tables defined by the hypervisor. Since modern operating systems maintain a set of page tables for every process, the shadow page tables will get flooded. Consequently, the perfor-mance overhead and cost of memory will be very high.

VMware uses shadow page tables to perform virtual-memory-to-machine-memory address translation. Processors use TLB hardware to map the virtual memory directly to the machine memory to avoid the two levels of translation on every access. When the guest OS changes the virtual memory to a physical memory mapping, the VMM updates the shadow page tables to enable a direct lookup. The AMD Barcelona processor has featured hardware-assisted memory virtualization since 2007. It provides hardware assistance to the two-stage address translation in a virtual execution environment by using a technology called nested paging.

Example: Extended Page Table by Intel for Memory Virtualization
Since the efficiency of the software shadow page table technique was too low, Intel developed a hardware-based EPT technique to improve it, as illustrated in Figure 3.13. In addition, Intel offers a Virtual Processor ID (VPID) to improve use of the TLB. Therefore, the performance of memory virtualization is greatly improved. In Figure, the page tables of the guest OS and EPT are all four-level.

When a virtual address needs to be translated, the CPU will first look for the L4 page table pointed to by Guest CR3. Since the address in Guest CR3 is a physical address in the guest OS, the CPU needs to convert the Guest CR3 GPA to the host physical address (HPA) using EPT. In this procedure, the CPU will check the EPT TLB to see if the translation is there. If there is no required translation in the EPT TLB, the CPU will look for it in the EPT. If the CPU cannot find the translation in the EPT, an EPT violation exception will be raised.

When the GPA of the L4 page table is obtained, the CPU will calculate the GPA of the L3 page table by using the GVA and the content of the L4 page table. If the entry corresponding to the GVA in the L4

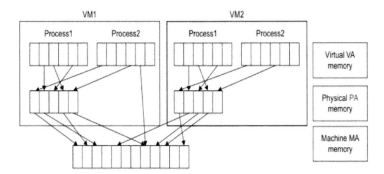

page table is a page fault, the CPU will generate a page fault interrupt and will let the guest OS kernel handle the interrupt. When the PGA of the L3 page table is obtained, the CPU will look for the EPT to get the HPA of the L3 page table, as described earlier. To get the HPA corresponding to a GVA, the CPU needs to look for the EPT five times, and each time, the memory needs to be accessed four times. There-fore, there are 20 memory accesses in the worst case, which is still very slow. To overcome this short-coming, Intel increased the size of the EPT

TLB to decrease the number of memory accesses.

I/O Virtualization

I/O virtualization involves managing the routing of I/O requests between virtual devices and the shared physical hardware. At the time of this writing, there are three ways to implement I/O virtualization: full device emulation, para-virtualization, and direct I/O. Full device emulation is the first approach for I/O virtualization. Generally, this approach emulates well-known, real-world devices.

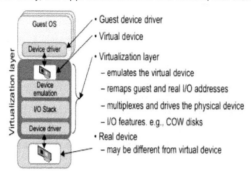

All the functions of a device or bus infrastructure, such as device enumeration, identification, interrupts, and DMA, are replicated in software. This software is located in the VMM and acts as a virtual device. The I/O access requests of the guest OS are trapped in the VMM which interacts with the I/O devices. The full device emulation approach is shown in Figure 3.14.

A single hardware device can be shared by multiple VMs that run concurrently. However, software emulation runs much slower than the hardware it emulates. The para-virtualization method of I/O virtualization is typically used in Xen. It is also known as the split driver model consisting of a frontend driver and a backend driver. The frontend driver is running in Domain U and the backend driver is running in Domain 0. They interact with each other via a block of shared memory. The frontend driver manages the I/O requests of the guest OSes and the backend driver is responsible for managing the real I/O devices and multiplexing the I/O data of different VMs. Although para-I/O-virtualization achieves better device performance than full device emulation, it comes with a higher CPU overhead.

Direct I/O virtualization lets the VM access devices directly. It can achieve close-to-native performance without high CPU costs. However, current direct I/O virtualization implementations focus on networking for mainframes. There are a lot of challenges for commodity hardware devices. For example, when a physical device is reclaimed (required by workload migration) for later reassign-ment, it may have been set to an arbitrary state (e.g., DMA to some arbitrary memory locations) that can function incorrectly or even crash the whole system. Since software-based I/O virtualization requires a very high overhead of device emulation, hardware-assisted I/O virtualization is critical. Intel VT-d supports the remapping of I/O DMA transfers and device-generated interrupts. The architecture of VT-d provides the flexibility to support multiple usage models that may run unmodified, special-purpose, or"virtualization-aware" guest OSes.

Another way to help I/O virtualization is via self-virtualized I/O (SV-IO) [47]. The key idea of SV-IO is to harness the rich resources of a multicore processor. All tasks associated with virtualizing an I/O device are encapsulated in SV-IO. It provides virtual devices and an associated access API to VMs and a management API to the VMM. SV-IO defines one virtual interface (VIF) for every kind of virtua-lized I/O device, such as virtual network interfaces, virtual block devices (disk), virtual camera devices, and others. The guest OS interacts with the VIFs via VIF device drivers. Each VIF consists of two mes-sage queues. One is for outgoing messages to the devices and the other is for incoming messages from the devices. In addition, each VIF has a unique ID for identifying it in SV-IO.

VIRTUALIZATION & DISASTER RECOVERY (DR)

Server virtualization has some interesting implications for DR and I think it has driven a lot of organizations to consider it more seriously over the past few years. Now more organizations are looking at server virtualization at primary and remote sites to ease server configuration issues and optimize the use of DR site resources as well. More organizations do this with DR in mind because of TCO-lowering DR management tools like VMware Inc. Site Recovery Manager. This allows easier management testing if you're using virtualization at both sites and can increase flexibility and the amount of use of the remote site when you're not using it to support a disaster.

So, when you move into a server virtualization environment at your primary site, server images become much more portable because they're not tied to specific hardware any longer, they're now encapsulated in this server virtualization environment. That server virtualization environment becomes the same at the remote site, regardless of the dissimilarities in underlying hardware.
As long as you have your host environment, your VMware ESX Server or your Microsoft Corp. Hyper-V Server set up right, that hardware is going to appear the same as the virtual image. I also think part of this is behavioral because server virtualization encourages us to separate data from virtual server boot volumes and encourages us to SAN-attach our virtualization environment in order to make more use of server virtualization features like moving host images back and forth across hardware.

When virtual images are stored on a SAN, it's easier to move them across hardware to get a load-balanced environment. Then, when they're on a SAN, it's easier to make better use of data protection and replication tools like snapshots. These can be array-based from a storage vendor like IBM Corp., Hewlett-Packard (HP) Co., Compellent, 3PAR Inc., EqualLogic, LeftHand Networks Inc. Or, these tools could even be from a heterogeneous storage virtualization vendor like DataCore Software Corp., IBM or FalconStor Software.

Some of these tools even offer broader reaching features, including their own functionality such as snapshots and replication, or they can be single point management. One example is DataCore. That product can even port virtual images from one format to another and allow you to protect your ESX environment with Hyper-V at another location. That might be cost-optimal for you. That's an extreme example and you're likely to face some compatibility issues, but there are other features to be had on top of these snapshot and replication tools. Regardless, in moving to server virtualization, you can harness all the capabilities of your storage environment, replication tools and snapshot tools. You can also ease the copy of data to your DR site to get closer to the moment before your disaster happens and make sure your data and remote site has more integrity.

Recover to any hardware

By using a virtualized environment you don't have to worry about having completely redundant hardware. Instead you can use almost any x86 platform as a backup solution, this allows you to save money by repurposing existing hardware and also gives your company more agility when it comes to hardware failure as almost any virtual server can be restarted on different hardware.

Backup and restore full images

By having your system completely virtualized each of your server's files are encapsulated in a single image file. An image is basically a single file that contains all of server's files, including system files, programs, and data; all in one location. By having these images it makes managing your systems easy and backups become as simple as duplicating the image file and restores are simplified to simply mounting the image on a new server.

Run other workloads on standby hardware

A key benefit to virtualization is reducing the hardware needed by utilizing your existing hardware more efficiently. This frees up systems that can now be used to run other tasks or be used as a hardware redundancy. This mixed with features like VMware's High Availability, which restarts a virtual machine on a different server when the original hardware fails, or for a more robust disaster recovery plan you can use Fault Tolerance, which keeps both servers in sync with each other leading to zero downtime if a server should fail.

Easily copy system data to recovery site

Having an offsite backup is a huge advantage if something were to happen to your specific location, whether it be a natural disaster, a power outage, or a water pipe bursting, it is nice to have all your information at an offsite location. Virtualization makes this easy by easily copying each virtual machines image to the offsite location and with the easy customizable automation process, it doesn't add any more strain or man hours to the IT department.

## 3

Cloud Computing Architecture

Cloud Architecture

Let's have a look into Cloud Computing and see what Cloud Computing is made of. Cloud computing comprises of two components front end and back end. Front end consist client part of cloud computing system. It comprise of interfaces and applications that are required to access the cloud computing platform.

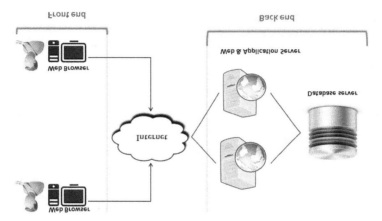

While back end refers to the cloud itself, it comprises of the resources that are required for cloud computing services. It consists of virtual machines, servers, data storage, security mechanism etc. It is under providers control.

Cloud computing distributes the file system that spreads over multiple hard disks and machines. Data is never stored in one place only and in case one unit fails the other will take over automatically. The user disk space is allocated on the distributed file system, while another important component is algorithm for resource allocation. Cloud computing is a strong distributed environment and it heavily depends upon strong algorithm.

The cloud services can be categorized into *software services* and *infrastructure or hardware services*. In terms of maturity, software in the cloud is much more evolved than hardware in the cloud.

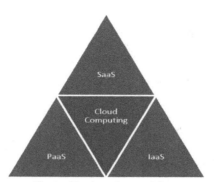
Figure:.Cloud service models

Cloud Software as a Service (SaaS) is basically a term that refers to software in the cloud. It represents the capability provided to the consumer to use the provider's applications running on a cloud infrastructure. The applications are accessible from various client devices through an interface such as a web browser (e.g. web-based email like Gmail is a form of SaaS provided by Google). The consumer does not manage or control the underlying cloud infrastructure including network, servers, operating systems, storage, or even individual application capabilities.

SaaS systems have some defining characteristics:
Availability via web browser
SaaS software never requires the installation of software on your laptop or desktop. You access it through a web browser using open standards or a browser plug-in.

On-demand availability
You should not have to go through a sales process to gain access to SaaS-based software. Once you have access, you should be able to go back into the software any time, from anywhere.

Payment terms based on usage
SaaS does not need any infrastructure investment or complex setup, so you should not have to pay any massive setup fees. You should simply pay for the parts of the service you use as you use them. When you no longer need those services, you simply stop paying.

Minimal IT demands
SaaS systems don't require a high technical knowledge for their configuration.

Cloud Platform as a Service (PaaS). The capability provided to the consumer is to deploy onto the cloud infrastructure consumer-created or acquired applications created using programming languages and tools supported by the provider. The consumer does not manage or control the underlying cloud infrastructure, but has control over the deployed applications and possibly application hosting environment configurations.

Cloud Infrastructure as a Service (IaaS). The capability provided to the consumer is to make use of processing, storage, networks, and other fundamental computing resources where the consumer is able to deploy and run arbitrary software, which can include operating systems and applications. The consumer does not manage or control the underlying cloud infrastructure but has control over operating systems, storage, deployed applications.

Infrastructure as a Service (IaaS)

The focus of this tutorial is on the IaaS service model. Amazon Web Services (AWS) is one of the major players in this area. The AWS is based on pure virtualization, it owns all the hardware and controls the network infrastructure and you own everything from the guest operating system up. You request virtual instances on- demand and let them go when you are done.

AppNexus represents a different approach to this problem. As with AWS, AppNexus enables you to gain access to servers on demand. However, it provides dedicated servers with virtualization on top. You have the confidence in knowing that your applications are not fighting with anyone else for resources and that you can meet any requirements that demand full control over all physical server resources.

Hybrid computing takes advantage of both approaches, offering virtualization when appropriate and a dedicated hardware when appropriate. In addition, most hybrid vendors such as Rackspace [4] and GoGrid [5] base their model on the idea that users still want a traditional data center and dedicated storage, but they just want it in the cloud.

This text focuses on the Amazon AWS and provides a practical example about using the Amazon EC2 IaaS solution.

Amazon Web Services (AWS)

AWS is Amazon's umbrella description of all of their web-based technology services. It encompasses a wide variety of services, all of which fall into the concept of cloud computing like:

Amazon Elastic Cloud Compute (Amazon EC2)
Amazon Simple Storage Service (Amazon S3)
Amazon Simple Queue Service (Amazon SQS)
Amazon CloudFront
Amazon SimpleDB
Amazon Elastic Cloud Computing (EC2)

Amazon EC2 is the heart of the Amazon cloud. It provides a web services API for provisioning, managing, and de-provisioning of virtual servers inside the Amazon cloud. In other words, any application anywhere on the Internet can launch a virtual server in the Amazon cloud with a single web services call.

At the time of this tutorial, Amazon's EC2 U.S. footprint has three data centers on the east coast of the U.S. and two in western Europe. You can sign up separately for an Amazon European data center account, but you cannot mix U.S.

and European environments. The servers in these environments run a highly customized version of tools that are using the virtualization concept and enable the dynamic provisioning and de-provisioning of servers. When you want to start up a virtual server in the Amazon environment, you launch a new instance based on a predefined *Amazon machine image* (AMI). The AMI includes your operating system and any other prebuilt software. Most people start with a standard AMI based on their favorite operating system, customize it, create a new image based on their preferences, and then launch their servers based on their custom images.

Many competitors to Amazon also provide persistent internal storage for nodes to make them operate more like a traditional data center.

In addition, servers in EC2 like any other server on the Internet can access Amazon S3 for cloud-based persistent storage. EC2 servers in particular achieve cost savings and greater efficiencies in accessing S3.

When most people think of the Amazon cloud, they are thinking about

Amazon EC2. EC2 represents your virtual network with all of the virtual servers running inside that network. When you use EC2, you will be able to use S3 to store your machine images and also for other storage needs.

Amazon EC2 Concepts
Amazon EC2 is a bit more complex than S3. Figure shows all of the concepts that make up Amazon EC2 and how they relate to each other.
The main concepts are:

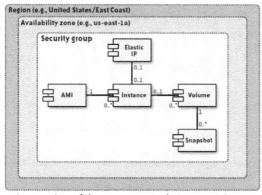

Figure: .An overview of the components that support Amazon EC2

Instance
An Amazon EC2 instance is a virtual server running your choice of guest operating system based on the machine image from which the instance was created.

Amazon Machine Image (AMI)

A copy of your server that you can use to launch any number of instances. If you are familiar with the concept of ghosting, the machine image represents your ghost image from which you can build any number of servers. Minimally, a machine image will have the core operating system plus common preinstalled tools. Amazon has some prebuilt AMIs to get you started easily.

Elastic IP address
This is simply a static IP address that is assigned to you. (The term "elastic" doesn't mean a dynamic address, it is a static one) By default, each Amazon instance comes with a dynamically assigned IP address that may be reassigned to another user when your instance terminates. Elastic IP addresses are reserved to you and thus useful for instances that must always be accessible by the same static IP address.

Region
A group of availability zones that form a single geographic cluster. Until now, Amazon's service level agreement (SLA) for EC2 guarantees 99.95% availability of at least two availability zones within a region over the course of a 12-month period .

Availability zone
Almost analogous to a data center. Amazon currently has three zones in the U.S., all on the east coast. It also has two zones in western Europe. You may optionally define the availability zone into which you launch your instances to create a level of location redundancy for your applications.

Security group
Very roughly analogous to a network segment protected by a firewall. You launch your instances into security groups and, in turn, the security groups define what can talk to your new instances and what is prohibited.

Block storage volume
Like a SAN (storage area network), it provides block-level storage that you can mount from your EC2 instances. You can then format the volume as you want, or write raw data to the volume.

Snapshot
You may take "snapshots" of your block volumes for backup or replication purposes. These snapshots are stored in Amazon S3, where they can be used to create new volumes.

Amazon EC2 Access
Like Amazon S3, the primary means of accessing Amazon EC2 is through a web services API. Amazon provides a number of interactive tools on top of their web services API, including:
o The Amazon Web Services Management Console
o The ElasticFox Firefox plug-in
o The Amazon Command Line tools

The example explained here focuses on using the management console which is one of the easiest and user friendly means.

Amazon EC2 step by step

In this section, you will learn how to create and use the Amazon EC2 instance in a step by step.

1. Open the Amazon EC2 web page http://aws.amazon.com/ec2/ and click the Get Started With Amazon EC2 button.

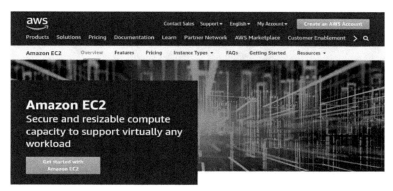

2. Register with you e-mail.

Sign up for AWS

Explore Free Tier products with a new AWS account.

To learn more, visit aws.amazon.com/free.

Email address
You will use this email address to sign in to your new AWS account.

Password

Confirm password

AWS account name
Choose a name for your account. You can change this name in your account settings after you sign up.

Continue (step 1 of 5)

3. Add your payment information taking into account that it will not be charged as we are using a free service, but it is mandatory to enter your payment information.

You'll be informed with a PIN number then; you'll get a phone call asking you to enter the PIN number to be identified correctly.

4. Click on launch Instance button.

5. Enter your new instance name and select one of the available configuration (in this tutorial we are using the free Ubuntu 12.04.1 LTS configuration)

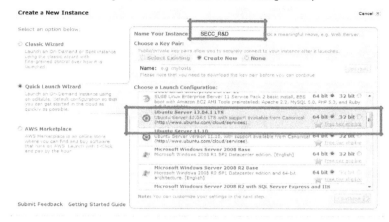

6. Enter the name of the .pem file, which is the identifier you'll need when connecting to the instance. After that click download button and save this .pem file in a secure path on your hard disk. When you finish click on the continue button

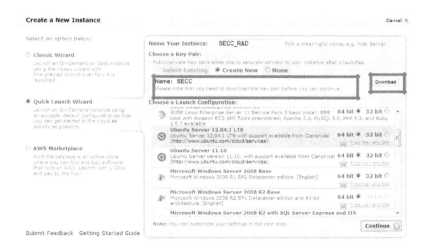

7. Click on the launch button

8.Click on Instances from the left pane.

You'll find your created instance as shown below and it is running by default

9. Configure your security options by clicking the security groups from the left pane and check the "quicklaunch-1" security configuration (Created by default).

10. Add the ports numbers of the most common applications in the port range entry one by one like:

Port 80 and 8080 for HTML applications

Port 21 for FTP

Port 3306 for MySQL server application

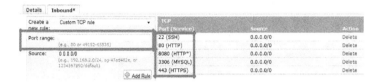

11. Select your instance by checking the corresponding check box then select Actions ->connect

12. Enter the user name (ubuntu) and add the path of your .pem file and then click "Launch SSH Client".
A new terminal will appear as if you are opening a terminal on a ubuntu machine.

By this way, we were able to use the Amazon EC2 IaaS technology to create a free ubuntu instance that acts as a server or computing unit for development and even commercial purposes. You can use it for hosting your website/web services or performing any processing required for your applications.

4

RESOURCE MANAGEMENT AND SECURITY IN CLOUD

It is the responsibility of cloud provider to manage resources and their performance. Management of resources includes several aspects of cloud computing such as load balancing, performance, storage, backups, capacity, deployment, etc. The management is essential to access full functionality of resources in the cloud.

Cloud Management Tasks

The cloud provider performs a number of tasks to ensure efficient use of cloud resources. Here, we will discuss some of them:

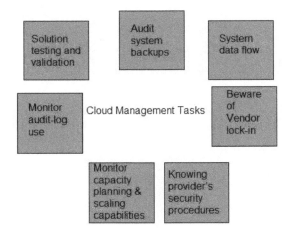

Audit System Backups

It is required to audit the backups timely to ensure restoring of randomly selected files of different users. Backups can be performed in following ways:

- Backing up files by the company, from on-site computers to the disks that reside within the cloud.

- Backing up files by the cloud provider.

It is necessary to know if cloud provider has encrypted the data, who has access to that data and if the backup is taken at different locations then the user must know the details of those locations.

Data Flow of the System

The managers are responsible to develop a diagram describing a detailed process flow. This process flow describes the movement of data belonging to an organization throughout the cloud solution.

Vendor Lock-In Awareness and Solutions

The managers must know the procedure to exit from services of a particular cloud provider. The procedures must be defined to enable the cloud managers to export data of an organization from their system to another cloud provider.

Knowing Provider's Security Procedures

The managers should know the security plans of the provider for the following services:

- Multitenant use

- E-commerce processing

- Employee screening

- Encryption policy

Monitoring Capacity Planning and Scaling Capabilities

The managers must know the capacity planning in order to ensure whether the cloud provider is meeting the future capacity requirement for his business or not.

The managers must manage the scaling capabilities in order to ensure services can be scaled up or down as per the user need.

Monitor Audit Log Use

In order to identify errors in the system, managers must audit the logs on a regular basis.

Solution Testing and Validation

When the cloud provider offers a solution, it is essential to test it in order to ensure that it gives the correct result and it is error-free. This is necessary for a system to be robust and reliable.

Cloud Computing Security

Security in cloud computing is a major concern. Data in cloud should be stored in encrypted form. To restrict client from accessing the shared data directly, proxy and brokerage services should be employed.

Security Planning

Before deploying a particular resource to cloud, one should need to analyze several aspects of the resource such as:

- Select resource that needs to move to the cloud and analyze its sensitivity to risk.

- Consider cloud service models such as IaaS, PaaS,and SaaS. These models require customer to be responsible for security at different levels of service.

- Consider the cloud type to be used such as public, private, community or hybrid.

- Understand the cloud service provider's system about data storage and its transfer into and out of the cloud.

The risk in cloud deployment mainly depends upon the service models and cloud types.

Understanding Security of Cloud

Security Boundaries

A particular service model defines the boundary between the responsibilities of service provider and customer. Cloud Security Alliance (CSA) stack model defines the boundaries between each service model and shows how different functional units relate to each other. The following diagram shows the CSA stack model:

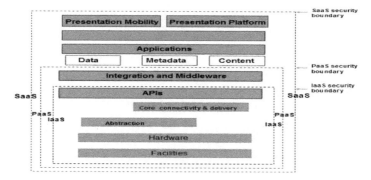

Key Points to CSA Model

- IaaS is the most basic level of service with PaaS and SaaS next two above levels of services.

- Moving upwards, each of the service inherits capabilities and security concerns of the model beneath.

- IaaS provides the infrastructure, PaaS provides platform development environment, and SaaS provides operating environment.

- IaaS has the least level of integrated functionalities and integrated security while SaaS has the most.

- This model describes the security boundaries at which cloud service provider's responsibilities end and the customer's responsibilities begin.

- Any security mechanism below the security boundary must be built into the system and should be maintained by the customer.

Although each service model has security mechanism, the security needs also depend upon where these services are located, in private, public, hybrid or community cloud.

Understanding Data Security

Since all the data is transferred using Internet, data security is of major concern in the cloud. Here are key mechanisms for protecting data.

- Access Control

- Auditing

- Authentication

- Authorization

All of the service models should incorporate security mechanism operating in all above-mentioned areas.

Isolated Access to Data

Since data stored in cloud can be accessed from anywhere, we must have a mechanism to isolate data and protect it from client's direct access.

Brokered Cloud Storage Access is an approach for isolating storage in the cloud. In this approach, two services are created:

- A broker with full access to storage but no access to client.
- A proxy with no access to storage but access to both client and broker.

Working Of Brokered Cloud Storage Access System

When the client issues request to access data:

- The client data request goes to the external service interface of proxy.
- The proxy forwards the request to the broker.
- The broker requests the data from cloud storage system.
- The cloud storage system returns the data to the broker.
- The broker returns the data to proxy.
- Finally the proxy sends the data to the client.

All of the above steps are shown in the following diagram:

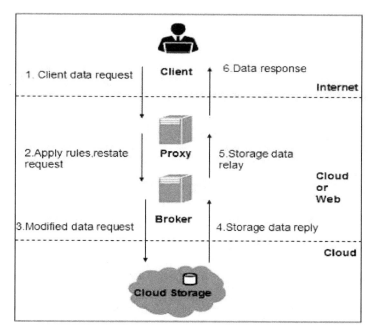

Encryption

Encryption helps to protect data from being compromised. It protects data that is being transferred as well as data stored in the cloud. Although encryption helps to protect data from any unauthorized access, it does not prevent data loss.

Privacy Concern & Cloud Computing
Privacy present a strong barrier for users to adapt into Cloud Computing systems There are certain measures which can improve privacy in cloud computing.

1.   The administrative staff of the cloud computing service could theoretically monitor the data moving in memory before it is stored in disk.To keep the confidentiality of a data, administrative and legal controls should prevent this from happening.
2.   The other way for increasing the privacy is to keep the data encrypted at the cloud storage site, preventing unauthorized access through the internet; even cloud vendor can't access the data either.

5

Auditing Framework for Cloud Computing Environment

The purpose of this chapter is to present different aspects of designing an auditing framework for Cloud Computing Environment (CCE). Data security becomes the most significant issue in all levels of services such as IAAS, PAAS, SAAS. Audit in CCE provides the way for Cloud Service Provider to make their performance and data readily available for the cloud user. Auditing ensures integrity of the sensitive data and restricted access of computing and physical resources. This chapter aim to present an auditing framework that helps the designer to incorporate different challenges of auditing in CCE.

Role of Third Party Service Provider in Auditing

In the surge of rapid usage of internet over the world, several security issues are concerned such as handling web attacks [40], data access control, enhancing dynamic allocation strategies, and controlling sensitive information flow. According to Information Systems Control and Audit, IT auditing can be defined as a process of aggregating and evaluating evidence to decide whether a computing information system safeguards resources, maintains data integrity and secure sensitive user data, attains organizational objectives effectively and consumes physical and computing resources efficiently. Information assurance controls in Governing documents like DoDI 8500.2, NIST SP800-53 or Common Criteria have supported auditing by dictating minimal requirements for audit considering the fact that ensures proper access control such as authorization, authentication and auditing to the physical and virtual resources used at public cloud provider. It is also necessary to ensure the availability of the Internet-facing resources in a public cloud being used by the organization. At the host level of security, virtualization security threats like system configuration change, weak access control of the hypervisor, faulty provisioning of resources, proper use of VM instances are to be considered for making secure cloud. The integrity and availability of the hypervisor is to be guaranteed because a vulnerable hypervisor could expose all user domains to malicious insiders. Security controls are to be maintained for platform level (PaaS) applications where user authentication, account management, endpoint security measures including antivirus, and browser with latest patches are to be authorized. Security issues and different negotiation protocols are concerned with auditing. Audibility also enables accountability (retrospective). It allows taking an action to be reviewed against a pre-determined policy. In public auditing, the cloud user takes the assistance of a Third Party Auditor (TPA) for integrity checking of stored data in cloud. The TPA checks the integrity of data on user demand and the released audit reports help the user to evaluate the risk of their services.

Auditing Framework

An auditing framework is a coordinated system of tools and behaviour in order to audit the data, regulation, risk and security in cloud. The framework processes a model with respect to time, effort, policy, technology, security aspects and provides an effective environment to estimate the risk of security in Cloud Computing Environment.

Considering Cloud data storage scenario as given in Figure, I have proposed the framework for auditing for cloud which consists of four entities namely:

Cloud User or Cloud Subscriber who may either deploy its application or use the Cloud services or use the cloud data storage.

Service Broker which maintains the relations between Business Service Provider Layer and Virtual Appliances layer has the responsibility to manage the user-applications.

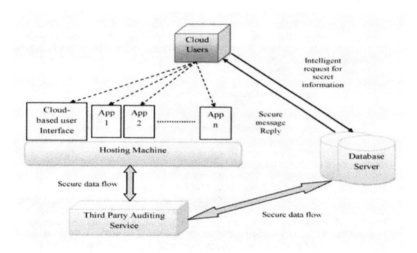

Hosting Service or *Cloud Service Provider* (CSP) provides infrastructure elements for metered usage, service level policy and license management, and authentication control.

Auditing Service which maintains the confidentiality of the sensitive data, restricted access of computing and physical resources and to check integrity

Figure represents the work flow of the proposed auditing framework in terms of individual components description and communication among those components as described below:

Service Broker

Cloud user who wants to deploy its application or to use the service is required to register itself in the broker server that facilitates services like register, request, monitor and manage. So that the service broker can maintain the user-log in the log server and can deliver it to the auditing service. The major aim of the service broker is to arrange the applications optimally so that it can easily monitor the requests of applications and can manage the configuration of the platforms. Then the deployment request is being delivered to the hosting service. While handling the request, we have to consider a directory service which acts as a depository for the credential, identity, and user attributes of the users of the organization. This directory service directly interacts with Identification Management Service (IMS) and Authentication Access Management Service (AAMS).

Identification Management Service (IMS)

IMS technology consists of life cycle management module, creation of validation module and provisioning module. Life cycle management module identifies different phases when an organization is renting the Cloud infrastructure from the CSPs or going to deploy its user-application onto a cloud. Creation of validation module identifies the proper validation for deployment of user-application. Provisioning is the process which provides users with essential access to data and technology resources. Hence this module is responsible for identification of proper provisioning of resources.

Authentication and Access Management Service (AAMS)

AAMS comprises of identification and authentication management service, user management service, data management and provisioning service, and access control service module. Identification and authentication management service is responsible for effective governance and management of the proper process. User management service is associated with the rules and policies, and management of identifying life cycles. Data management and provisioning service is responsible for propagation of identifying data for authorization to IT resources. Access management and access control service module enables the rules and policies for access control in response to a request from any user or services which are in need of IT resources within the organization. Access control service is also responsible for user access management, user responsibilities, network access control, and operating system access control. Policy validation is the important module for validating and implementing the policies.

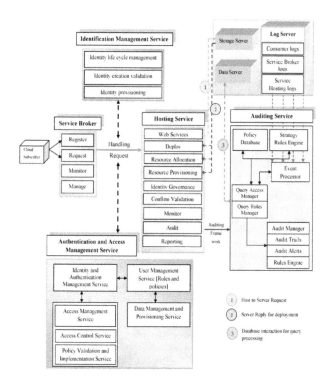

Hosting Service

In Cloud Service Provider, hosting service consists of different modules. Web services are meant for interfaces through which users and service brokers interact with the service providers. When all the identification and authentication are done, user application is deployed onto the host machine and host machine make a request for physical resources from Infrastructure as a Service (IaaS) layer through Virtual Machine Manager (VMM) or hypervisor. Then the infrastructure layer allocates the necessary resources for the particular application and physical & virtual resources are immediately provisioned according to the need of the user. In this workflow, identity governance is essentially needed for recognizing virtual machine ID and datacenter ID so that the host machine can easily identify the proper request related concerns. After verifying the identifications, host machine confirms the validation for resource allocation. Monitoring, auditing, and reporting compliance by cloud subscribers regarding access to a pool of physical resources like servers, networks, bandwidth, storage, and data center space within the organization depend upon the defined policies. Monitoring service is also responsible for detecting unauthorized information processing activities. After this, auditing service plays an important role to ensure security of the user data and application related concerns.

Auditing Service

Auditing Service consists of Policy database, Strategy rules engine, Event processor, Query manager having two modules like Query access manager and Query rules manager, and Audit control module comprising of Audit manager, Audit trails, Audit alerts and Rules engine. Policy database is the repository of information security policies that provide management direction and support for information security according to the business requirements and relevant laws, policies and regulations. Strategy rules engine defines the strategy plan for the implementation of security policy, asset management, communications and operational management, information systems acquisition & development & maintenance, and business continuity management. Event processor is the most important module in auditing service. Event processor is associated with the dynamic change in the user-events and related with the log server. Log server comprises of consumer logs having details of cloud subscriber details like user ID, usage time etc., service broker logs containing broker ID and broker details, and service hosting logs having virtual machine ID, datacenter ID, resource usage, storage details etc. Event processor, maintaining all the log tables from log server, also has the authority to set the priority to the events and process activities. Query Access manager manages and controls the access of query processing unit in authorized way and query rules manager set the rules for query processing. These two modules directly interact with the database server for query processing. While processing the database query, it is in need of query audit. Audit manager manages the overall Auditing process, whereas audit trails have the responsibilities to trace the unauthorized query and audit alert makes an alert in case of unauthorized query access. Therefore, a set of auditing rules and query accessing policies are made by rules engine. The Cloud Computing Environment enables its customers to dynamically aggregate and change for the services provided by the service providers. Due to this dynamic nature of Cloud, the Cloud Service provider may lose the control over sensitive as well as personal data. Hence while designing an auditing framework for cloud, security issues like confidentiality, integrity, authentication and non-repudiation can be taken care by the designer.

Our proposed auditing framework reflects the communication among all cloud actors namely cloud user, cloud broker, Cloud Service Provider and cloud auditor which gives a brief idea of different security issues in CCE. Our proposed auditing framework addresses the importance of authentication and non-repudiation in CCE through Identification Management Service(IMS) and Authentication and Access Management Service (AAMS) module which are not addressed by existing auditing frameworks for cloud.

6

Cloud Computing Technologies & Advancements

Hadoop - Introduction

Hadoop is an Apache open source framework written in java that allows distributed processing of large datasets across clusters of computers using simple programming models. A Hadoop frame-worked application works in an environment that provides distributed storage and computation across clusters of computers. Hadoop is designed to scale up from single server to thousands of machines, each offering local computation and storage.

Hadoop Architecture

Hadoop framework includes following four modules:

- **Hadoop Common:** These are Java libraries and utilities required by other Hadoop modules. These libraries provides filesystem and OS level abstractions and contains the necessary Java files and scripts required to start Hadoop.

- **Hadoop YARN:** This is a framework for job scheduling and cluster resource management.

- **Hadoop Distributed File System (HDFS™):** A distributed file system that provides high-throughput access to application data.

- **Hadoop MapReduce:** This is YARN-based system for parallel processing of large data sets.

We can use following diagram to depict these four components available in Hadoop framework.

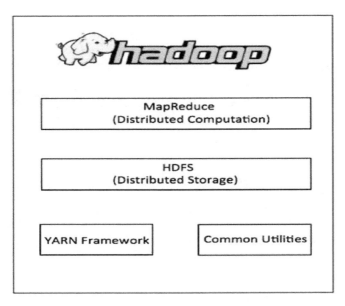

Since 2012, the term "Hadoop" often refers not just to the base modules mentioned above but also to the collection of additional software packages that can be installed on top of or alongside Hadoop, such as Apache Pig, Apache Hive, Apache HBase, Apache Spark etc.

MapReduce

Hadoop **MapReduce** is a software framework for easily writing applications which process big amounts of data in-parallel on large clusters (thousands of nodes) of commodity hardware in a reliable, fault-tolerant manner.

The term MapReduce actually refers to the following two different tasks that Hadoop programs perform:

- **The Map Task:** This is the first task, which takes input data and converts it into a set of data, where individual elements are broken down into tuples (key/value pairs).

- **The Reduce Task:** This task takes the output from a map task as input and combines those data tuples into a smaller set of tuples. The reduce task is always performed after the map task.

Typically both the input and the output are stored in a file-system. The framework takes care of scheduling tasks, monitoring them and re-executes the failed tasks.

The MapReduce framework consists of a single master **JobTracker** and one slave **TaskTracker** per cluster-node. The master is responsible for resource management, tracking resource consumption/availability and scheduling the jobs component tasks on the slaves, monitoring them and re-executing the failed tasks. The slaves TaskTracker execute the tasks as directed by the master and provide task-status information to the master periodically.

The JobTracker is a single point of failure for the Hadoop MapReduce service which means if JobTracker goes down, all running jobs are halted.

Hadoop Distributed File System

Hadoop can work directly with any mountable distributed file system such as Local FS, HFTP FS, S3 FS, and others, but the most common file system used by Hadoop is the Hadoop Distributed File System (HDFS).

The Hadoop Distributed File System (HDFS) is based on the Google File System (GFS) and provides a distributed file system that is designed to run on large clusters (thousands of computers) of small computer machines in a reliable, fault-tolerant manner.

HDFS uses a master/slave architecture where master consists of a single **NameNode** that manages the file system metadata and one or more slave **DataNodes** that store the actual data.

A file in an HDFS namespace is split into several blocks and those blocks are stored in a set of DataNodes. The NameNode determines the mapping of blocks to the DataNodes. The DataNodes takes care of read and write operation with the file system. They also take care of block creation, deletion and replication based on instruction given by NameNode.

HDFS provides a shell like any other file system and a list of commands are available to interact with the file system. These shell commands will be covered in a separate chapter along with appropriate examples.

How Does Hadoop Work?

Stage 1

A user/application can submit a job to the Hadoop (a hadoop job client) for required process by specifying the following items:

1. The location of the input and output files in the distributed file system.

2. The java classes in the form of jar file containing the implementation of map and reduce functions.

3. The job configuration by setting different parameters specific to the job.

Stage 2

The Hadoop job client then submits the job (jar/executable etc) and configuration to the JobTracker which then assumes the responsibility of distributing the software/configuration to the slaves, scheduling tasks and monitoring them, providing status and diagnostic information to the job-client.

Stage 3

The TaskTrackers on different nodes execute the task as per MapReduce implementation and output of the reduce function is stored into the output files on the file system.

Advantages of Hadoop

- Hadoop framework allows the user to quickly write and test distributed systems. It is efficient, and it automatic distributes the data and work across the machines and in turn, utilizes the underlying parallelism of the CPU cores.

- Hadoop does not rely on hardware to provide fault-tolerance and high availability (FTHA), rather Hadoop library itself has been designed to detect and handle failures at the application layer.

- Servers can be added or removed from the cluster dynamically and Hadoop continues to operate without interruption.

- Another big advantage of Hadoop is that apart from being open source, it is compatible on all the platforms since it is Java based.

Hadoop - Enviornment Setup

Hadoop is supported by GNU/Linux platform and its flavors. Therefore, we have to install a Linux operating system for setting up Hadoop environment. In case you have an OS other than Linux, you can install a Virtualbox software in it and have Linux inside the Virtualbox.

Pre-installation Setup

Before installing Hadoop into the Linux environment, we need to set up Linux using ssh (Secure Shell). Follow the steps given below for setting up the Linux environment.

Creating a User

At the beginning, it is recommended to create a separate user for Hadoop to isolate Hadoop file system from Unix file system. Follow the steps given below to create a user:

- Open the root using the command "su".

- Create a user from the root account using the command "useradd username".

- Now you can open an existing user account using the command "su username".

Open the Linux terminal and type the following commands to create a user.

```
$ su
 password:
# useradd hadoop
# passwd hadoop
 New passwd:
 Retype new passwd
```

SSH Setup and Key Generation

SSH setup is required to do different operations on a cluster such as starting, stopping, distributed daemon shell operations. To authenticate different users of Hadoop, it is required to provide public/private key pair for a Hadoop user and share it with different users.

The following commands are used for generating a key value pair using SSH. Copy the public keys form id_rsa.pub to authorized_keys, and provide the owner with read and write permissions to authorized_keys file respectively.

```
$ ssh-keygen -t rsa
$ cat ~/.ssh/id_rsa.pub >> ~/.ssh/authorized_keys
$ chmod 0600 ~/.ssh/authorized_keys
```

Installing Java

Java is the main prerequisite for Hadoop. First of all, you should verify the existence of java in your system using the command "java -version". The syntax of java version command is given below.

```
$ java -version
```

If everything is in order, it will give you the following output.

```
java version "1.7.0_71"
```

Java(TM) SE Runtime Environment (build 1.7.0_71-b13)

Java HotSpot(TM) Client VM (build 25.0-b02, mixed mode)

If java is not installed in your system, then follow the steps given below for installing java.

Step 1

Download java (JDK <latest version> - X64.tar.gz) by visiting the following linkhttp://www.oracle.com/technetwork/java/javase/downloads/jdk7-downloads1880260.html.

Then jdk-7u71-linux-x64.tar.gz will be downloaded into your system.

Step 2

Generally you will find the downloaded java file in Downloads folder. Verify it and extract the jdk-7u71-linux-x64.gz file using the following commands.

```
$ cd Downloads/
$ ls
jdk-7u71-linux-x64.gz
$ tar zxf jdk-7u71-linux-x64.gz
$ ls
jdk1.7.0_71   jdk-7u71-linux-x64.gz
```

Step 3

To make java available to all the users, you have to move it to the location "/usr/local/". Open root, and type the following commands.

```
$ su
password:
# mv jdk1.7.0_71 /usr/local/
# exit
```

Step 4

For setting up PATH and JAVA_HOME variables, add the following commands to ~/.bashrc file.

```
export JAVA_HOME=/usr/local/jdk1.7.0_71
export PATH=$PATH:$JAVA_HOME/bin
```

Now apply all the changes into the current running system.

```
$ source ~/.bashrc
```

Step 5

Use the following commands to configure java alternatives:

```
# alternatives --install /usr/bin/java java usr/local/java/bin/java 2
# alternatives --install /usr/bin/javac javac usr/local/java/bin/javac 2
# alternatives --install /usr/bin/jar jar usr/local/java/bin/jar 2
# alternatives --set java usr/local/java/bin/java
# alternatives --set javac usr/local/java/bin/javac
# alternatives --set jar usr/local/java/bin/jar
```

Now verify the java -version command from the terminal as explained above.

Downloading Hadoop

Download and extract Hadoop 2.4.1 from Apache software foundation using the following commands.

```
$ su
password:
# cd /usr/local
# wget http://apache.claz.org/hadoop/common/hadoop-2.4.1/
hadoop-2.4.1.tar.gz
# tar xzf hadoop-2.4.1.tar.gz
# mv hadoop-2.4.1/* to hadoop/
# exit
```

Hadoop Operation Modes

Once you have downloaded Hadoop, you can operate your Hadoop cluster in one of the three supported modes:

- **Local/Standalone Mode** : After downloading Hadoop in your system, by default, it is configured in a standalone mode and can be run as a single java process.

- **Pseudo Distributed Mode** : It is a distributed simulation on single machine. Each Hadoop daemon such as hdfs, yarn, MapReduce etc., will run as a separate java process. This mode is useful for development.

- **Fully Distributed Mode** : This mode is fully distributed with minimum two or more machines as a cluster. We will come across this mode in detail in the coming chapters.

Installing Hadoop in Standalone Mode

Here we will discuss the installation of **Hadoop 2.4.1** in standalone mode.

There are no daemons running and everything runs in a single JVM. Standalone mode is suitable for running MapReduce programs during development, since it is easy to test and debug them.

Setting Up Hadoop

You can set Hadoop environment variables by appending the following commands to ~/.**bashrc** file.

```
export HADOOP_HOME=/usr/local/hadoop
```

Before proceeding further, you need to make sure that Hadoop is working fine. Just issue the following command:

```
$ hadoop version
```

If everything is fine with your setup, then you should see the following result:

```
Hadoop 2.4.1
Subversion https://svn.apache.org/repos/asf/hadoop/common -r 1529768
Compiled by hortonmu on 2013-10-07T06:28Z
Compiled with protoc 2.5.0
From source with checksum 79e53ce7994d1628b240f09af91e1af4
```

It means your Hadoop's standalone mode setup is working fine. By default, Hadoop is configured to run in a non-distributed mode on a single machine.

Example

Let's check a simple example of Hadoop. Hadoop installation delivers the following example MapReduce jar file, which provides basic functionality of MapReduce and can be used for calculating, like Pi value, word counts in a given list of files, etc.

```
$HADOOP_HOME/share/hadoop/mapreduce/hadoop-mapreduce-examples-
2.2.0.jar
```

Let's have an input directory where we will push a few files and our requirement is to count the total number of words in those files. To calculate the total number of words, we do not need to write our MapReduce, provided the .jar file contains the implementation for word count. You can try other examples using the same .jar file; just issue the following commands to check supported MapReduce functional programs by hadoop-mapreduce-examples-2.2.0.jar file.

```
$ hadoop jar $HADOOP_HOME/share/hadoop/mapreduce/hadoop-mapreduceexamples-2.2.0.jar
```

Step 1

Create temporary content files in the input directory. You can create this input directory anywhere you would like to work.

```
$ mkdir input
$ cp $HADOOP_HOME/*.txt input
$ ls -l input
```

It will give the following files in your input directory:

```
total 24
-rw-r--r-- 1 root root 15164 Feb 21 10:14 LICENSE.txt
-rw-r--r-- 1 root root   101 Feb 21 10:14 NOTICE.txt
-rw-r--r-- 1 root root  1366 Feb 21 10:14 README.txt
```

These files have been copied from the Hadoop installation home directory. For your experiment, you can have different and large sets of files.

Step 2

Let's start the Hadoop process to count the total number of words in all the files available in the input directory, as follows:

```
$  hadoop  jar  $HADOOP_HOME/share/hadoop/mapreduce/hadoop-mapreduceexamples-
2.2.0.jar  wordcount input output
```

Step 3

Step-2 will do the required processing and save the output in output/part-r00000 file, which you can check by using:

```
$cat output/*
```

It will list down all the words along with their total counts available in all the files available in the input directory.

```
"AS      4
"Contribution" 1
"Contributor" 1
"Derivative 1
"Legal 1
"License"     1
"License");   1
"Licensor"    1
"NOTICE"      1
"Not    1
"Object"      1
"Source"      1
"Work"   1
"You"    1
"Your")  1
"[]"     1
"control"     1
"printed      1
"submitted"   1
(50%)    1
(BIS),   1
(C)      1
(Don't)  1
(ECCN)   1
(INCLUDING    2
(INCLUDING,   2
.............
```

Installing Hadoop in Pseudo Distributed Mode

Follow the steps given below to install Hadoop 2.4.1 in pseudo distributed mode.

Step 1: Setting Up Hadoop

You can set Hadoop environment variables by appending the following commands to ~/.bashrc file.

```
export HADOOP_HOME=/usr/local/hadoop
export HADOOP_MAPRED_HOME=$HADOOP_HOME
export HADOOP_COMMON_HOME=$HADOOP_HOME
export HADOOP_HDFS_HOME=$HADOOP_HOME
export YARN_HOME=$HADOOP_HOME
export HADOOP_COMMON_LIB_NATIVE_DIR=$HADOOP_HOME/lib/native
export PATH=$PATH:$HADOOP_HOME/sbin:$HADOOP_HOME/bin
export HADOOP_INSTALL=$HADOOP_HOME
```

Now apply all the changes into the current running system.

```
$ source ~/.bashrc
```

Step 2: Hadoop Configuration

You can find all the Hadoop configuration files in the location "$HADOOP_HOME/etc/hadoop". It is required to make changes in those configuration files according to your Hadoop infrastructure.

```
$ cd $HADOOP_HOME/etc/hadoop
```

In order to develop Hadoop programs in java, you have to reset the java environment variables in **hadoop-env.sh** file by replacing JAVA_HOME value with the location of java in your system.

```
export JAVA_HOME=/usr/local/jdk1.7.0_71
```

The following are the list of files that you have to edit to configure Hadoop.

core-site.xml

The **core-site.xml** file contains information such as the port number used for Hadoop instance, memory allocated for the file system, memory limit for storing the data, and size of Read/Write buffers.

Open the core-site.xml and add the following properties in between <configuration>, </configuration> tags.

```
<configuration>
```

```
<property>
  <name>fs.default.name</name>
  <value>hdfs://localhost:9000</value>
</property>
</configuration>
```

hdfs-site.xml

The **hdfs-site.xml** file contains information such as the value of replication data, namenode path, and datanode paths of your local file systems. It means the place where you want to store the Hadoop infrastructure.

Let us assume the following data.

```
dfs.replication (data replication value) = 1
(In the below given path /hadoop/ is the user name.
hadoopinfra/hdfs/namenode is the directory created by hdfs file system.)
namenode path = //home/hadoop/hadoopinfra/hdfs/namenode
(hadoopinfra/hdfs/datanode is the directory created by hdfs file system.)
datanode path = //home/hadoop/hadoopinfra/hdfs/datanode
```

Open this file and add the following properties in between the <configuration> </configuration> tags in this file.

```
<configuration>
  <property>
    <name>dfs.replication</name>
    <value>1</value>
  </property>

  <property>
    <name>dfs.name.dir</name>
    <value>file:///home/hadoop/hadoopinfra/hdfs/namenode </value>
  </property>
```

```
<property>

  <name>dfs.data.dir</name>

  <value>file:///home/hadoop/hadoopinfra/hdfs/datanode </value>

</property>


</configuration>
```

Note: In the above file, all the property values are user-defined and you can make changes according to your Hadoop infrastructure.

yarn-site.xml

This file is used to configure yarn into Hadoop. Open the yarn-site.xml file and add the following properties in between the <configuration>, </configuration> tags in this file.

```
<configuration>

  <property>

    <name>yarn.nodemanager.aux-services</name>

    <value>mapreduce_shuffle</value>

  </property>

</configuration>
```

mapred-site.xml

This file is used to specify which MapReduce framework we are using. By default, Hadoop contains a template of yarn-site.xml. First of all, it is required to copy the file from **mapred-site.xml.template** to **mapred-site.xml** file using the following command.

```
$ cp mapred-site.xml.template mapred-site.xml
```

Open mapred-site.xml file and add the following properties in between the <configuration>, </configuration>tags in this file.

```
<configuration>

  <property>

    <name>mapreduce.framework.name</name>
```

```
    <value>yarn</value>
  </property>
</configuration>
```

Verifying Hadoop Installation

The following steps are used to verify the Hadoop installation.

Step 1: Name Node Setup

Set up the namenode using the command "hdfs namenode -format" as follows.

```
$ cd ~
$ hdfs namenode -format
```

The expected result is as follows.

```
10/24/14 21:30:55 INFO namenode.NameNode: STARTUP_MSG:
/************************************************************
STARTUP_MSG: Starting NameNode
STARTUP_MSG:  host = localhost/192.168.1.11
STARTUP_MSG:  args = [-format]
STARTUP_MSG:  version = 2.4.1
...
...
10/24/14 21:30:56 INFO common.Storage: Storage directory
/home/hadoop/hadoopinfra/hdfs/namenode has been successfully formatted.
10/24/14 21:30:56 INFO namenode.NNStorageRetentionManager: Going to
retain 1 images with txid >= 0
10/24/14 21:30:56 INFO util.ExitUtil: Exiting with status 0
10/24/14 21:30:56 INFO namenode.NameNode: SHUTDOWN_MSG:
/************************************************************
SHUTDOWN_MSG: Shutting down NameNode at localhost/192.168.1.11
************************************************************/
```

Step 2: Verifying Hadoop dfs

The following command is used to start dfs. Executing this command will start your Hadoop file system.

```
$ start-dfs.sh
```

The expected output is as follows:

```
10/24/14 21:37:56

Starting namenodes on [localhost]

localhost: starting namenode, logging to /home/hadoop/hadoop

2.4.1/logs/hadoop-hadoop-namenode-localhost.out

localhost: starting datanode, logging to /home/hadoop/hadoop

2.4.1/logs/hadoop-hadoop-datanode-localhost.out

Starting secondary namenodes [0.0.0.0]
```

Step 3: Verifying Yarn Script

The following command is used to start the yarn script. Executing this command will start your yarn daemons.

```
$ start-yarn.sh
```

The expected output as follows:

```
starting yarn daemons

starting resourcemanager, logging to /home/hadoop/hadoop

2.4.1/logs/yarn-hadoop-resourcemanager-localhost.out

localhost: starting nodemanager, logging to /home/hadoop/hadoop

2.4.1/logs/yarn-hadoop-nodemanager-localhost.out
```

Step 4: Accessing Hadoop on Browser

The default port number to access Hadoop is 50070. Use the following url to get Hadoop services on browser.

```
http://localhost:50070/
```

Step 5: Verify All Applications for Cluster

The default port number to access all applications of cluster is 8088. Use the following url to visit this service.

http://localhost:8088/

What is MapReduce?

MapReduce is a processing technique and a program model for distributed computing based on java. The MapReduce algorithm contains two important tasks, namely Map and Reduce. Map takes a set of data and converts it into another set of data, where individual elements are broken down into tuples (key/value pairs). Secondly, reduce task, which takes the output from a map as an input and combines those data tuples into a smaller set of tuples. As the sequence of the name MapReduce implies, the reduce task is always performed after the map job.

The major advantage of MapReduce is that it is easy to scale data processing over multiple computing nodes. Under the MapReduce model, the data processing primitives are called mappers and reducers. Decomposing a data processing application into mappers and reducers is sometimes nontrivial. But, once we write an application in the MapReduce form, scaling the application to run over hundreds, thousands, or even tens of thousands of machines in a cluster is merely a configuration change. This simple scalability is what has attracted many programmers to use the MapReduce model.

The Algorithm

- Generally MapReduce paradigm is based on sending the computer to where the data resides!

- MapReduce program executes in three stages, namely map stage, shuffle stage, and reduce stage.

  o **Map stage** : The map or mapper's job is to process the input data. Generally the input data is in the form of file or directory and is stored in the Hadoop file system (HDFS). The input file is passed to the mapper function line by line. The mapper processes the data and creates several small chunks of data.

  o **Reduce stage** : This stage is the combination of the **Shuffle** stage and the **Reduce** stage. The Reducer's job is to process the data that comes from the mapper. After processing, it produces a new set of output, which will be stored in the HDFS.

- During a MapReduce job, Hadoop sends the Map and Reduce tasks to the appropriate servers in the cluster.

- The framework manages all the details of data-passing such as issuing tasks, verifying task completion, and copying data around the cluster between the nodes.

- Most of the computing takes place on nodes with data on local disks that reduces the network traffic.

- After completion of the given tasks, the cluster collects and reduces the data to form an appropriate result, and sends it back to the Hadoop server.

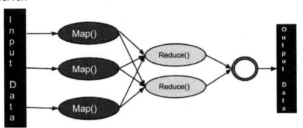

Inputs and Outputs (Java Perspective)

The MapReduce framework operates on <key, value> pairs, that is, the framework views the input to the job as a set of <key, value> pairs and produces a set of <key, value> pairs as the output of the job, conceivably of different types.

The key and the value classes should be in serialized manner by the framework and hence, need to implement the Writable interface. Additionally, the key classes have to implement the Writable-Comparable interface to facilitate sorting by the framework. Input and Output types of a MapReduce job: (Input) <k1, v1> -> map -> <k2, v2>-> reduce -> <k3, v3>(Output).

	Input	Output
Map	<k1, v1>	list (<k2, v2>)
Reduce	<k2, list(v2)>	list (<k3, v3>)

Terminology

- **PayLoad** - Applications implement the Map and the Reduce functions, and form the core of the job.

- **Mapper** - Mapper maps the input key/value pairs to a set of intermediate key/value pair.

- **NamedNode** - Node that manages the Hadoop Distributed File System (HDFS).

- **DataNode** - Node where data is presented in advance before any processing takes place.

- **MasterNode** - Node where JobTracker runs and which accepts job requests from clients.

- **SlaveNode** - Node where Map and Reduce program runs.

- **JobTracker** - Schedules jobs and tracks the assign jobs to Task tracker.

- **Task Tracker** - Tracks the task and reports status to JobTracker.

- **Job** - A program is an execution of a Mapper and Reducer across a dataset.

- **Task** - An execution of a Mapper or a Reducer on a slice of data.

- **Task Attempt** - A particular instance of an attempt to execute a task on a SlaveNode.

Example Scenario

Given below is the data regarding the electrical consumption of an organization. It contains the monthly electrical consumption and the annual average for various years.

	Jan	Feb	Mar	Apr	May	Jun	Jul	Aug	Sep	Oct	Nov	Dec	Avg
1979	23	23	2	43	24	25	26	26	26	26	25	26	25
1980	26	27	28	28	28	30	31	31	31	30	30	30	29
1981	31	32	32	32	33	34	35	36	36	34	34	34	34
1984	39	38	39	39	39	41	42	43	40	39	38	38	40
1985	38	39	39	39	39	41	41	41	00	40	39	39	45

If the above data is given as input, we have to write applications to process it and produce results such as finding the year of maximum usage, year of minimum usage, and so on. This is a walkover for the programmers with finite number of records. They will simply write the logic to produce the required output, and pass the data to the application written.

But, think of the data representing the electrical consumption of all the largescale industries of a particular state, since its formation.

When we write applications to process such bulk data,

- They will take a lot of time to execute.

- There will be a heavy network traffic when we move data from source to network server and so on.

To solve these problems, we have the MapReduce framework.

Input Data

The above data is saved as **sample.txt**and given as input. The input file looks as shown below.

1979	23	23	2	43	24	25	26	26	26	26	25	26	25
1980	26	27	28	28	28	30	31	31	31	30	30	30	29
1981	31	32	32	32	33	34	35	36	36	34	34	34	34
1984	39	38	39	39	39	41	42	43	40	39	38	38	40
1985	38	39	39	39	39	41	41	41	00	40	39	39	45

Example Program

Given below is the program to the sample data using MapReduce framework.

```
package hadoop;
import java.util.*;
import java.io.IOException;
import java.io.IOException;
import org.apache.hadoop.fs.Path;
import org.apache.hadoop.conf.*;
import org.apache.hadoop.io.*;
import org.apache.hadoop.mapred.*;
import org.apache.hadoop.util.*;
public class ProcessUnits
{
   //Mapper class
   public static class E_EMapper extends MapReduceBase implements
   Mapper<LongWritable ,/*Input key Type */
   Text,          /*Input value Type*/
```

```
Text,           /*Output key Type*/

IntWritable>       /*Output value Type*/

{

  //Map function

  public void map(LongWritable key, Text value,

  OutputCollector<Text, IntWritable> output,

  Reporter reporter) throws IOException

  {

    String line = value.toString();

    String lasttoken = null;

    StringTokenizer s = new StringTokenizer(line,"\t");

    String year = s.nextToken();

    while(s.hasMoreTokens())

      {

        lasttoken=s.nextToken();

      }

    int avgprice = Integer.parseInt(lasttoken);

    output.collect(new Text(year), new IntWritable(avgprice));

  }

}

//Reducer class

public static class E_EReduce extends MapReduceBase implements

Reducer< Text, IntWritable, Text, IntWritable >

{

  //Reduce function

  public void reduce( Text key, Iterator <IntWritable> values,

    OutputCollector<Text, IntWritable> output, Reporter reporter) throws
IOException

    {
```

```java
      int maxavg=30;
      int val=Integer.MIN_VALUE;
      while (values.hasNext())
      {
        if((val=values.next().get())>maxavg)
        {
          output.collect(key, new IntWritable(val));
        }
      }
    }
}


//Main function
public static void main(String args[])throws Exception
{
    JobConf conf = new JobConf(ProcessUnits.class);
    conf.setJobName("max_eletricityunits");
    conf.setOutputKeyClass(Text.class);
    conf.setOutputValueClass(IntWritable.class);
    conf.setMapperClass(E_EMapper.class);
    conf.setCombinerClass(E_EReduce.class);
    conf.setReducerClass(E_EReduce.class);
    conf.setInputFormat(TextInputFormat.class);
    conf.setOutputFormat(TextOutputFormat.class);
    FileInputFormat.setInputPaths(conf, new Path(args[0]));
    FileOutputFormat.setOutputPath(conf, new Path(args[1]));

    JobClient.runJob(conf);
}
```

}

Save the above program as **ProcessUnits.java**. The compilation and execution of the program is explained below.

Compilation and Execution of Process Units Program

Let us assume we are in the home directory of a Hadoop user (e.g. /home/hadoop).

Follow the steps given below to compile and execute the above program.

Step 1

The following command is to create a directory to store the compiled java classes.

```
$ mkdir units
```

Step 2

Download **Hadoop-core-1.2.1.jar,** which is used to compile and execute the MapReduce program. Visit the following link http://mvnrepository.com/artifact/org.apache.hadoop/hadoop-core/1.2.1 to download the jar. Let us assume the downloaded folder is **/home/hadoop/.**

Step 3

The following commands are used for compiling the **ProcessUnits.java** program and creating a jar for the program.

```
$ javac -classpath hadoop-core-1.2.1.jar -d units ProcessUnits.java
$ jar -cvf units.jar -C units/ .
```

Step 4

The following command is used to create an input directory in HDFS.

```
$HADOOP_HOME/bin/hadoop fs -mkdir input_dir
```

Step 5

The following command is used to copy the input file named **sample.txt**in the input directory of HDFS.

```
$HADOOP_HOME/bin/hadoop fs -put /home/hadoop/sample.txt input_dir
```

Step 6

The following command is used to verify the files in the input directory.

```
$HADOOP_HOME/bin/hadoop fs -ls input_dir/
```

Step 7

The following command is used to run the Eleunit_max application by taking the input files from the input directory.

$HADOOP_HOME/bin/hadoop   jar   units.jar   hadoop.ProcessUnits   input_dir output_dir

Wait for a while until the file is executed. After execution, as shown below, the output will contain the number of input splits, the number of Map tasks, the number of reducer tasks, etc.

INFO mapreduce.Job: Job job_1414748220717_0002

completed successfully

14/10/31 06:02:52

INFO mapreduce.Job: Counters: 49

File System Counters

FILE: Number of bytes read=61

FILE: Number of bytes written=279400

FILE: Number of read operations=0

FILE: Number of large read operations=0

FILE: Number of write operations=0

HDFS: Number of bytes read=546

HDFS: Number of bytes written=40

HDFS: Number of read operations=9

HDFS: Number of large read operations=0

HDFS: Number of write operations=2 Job Counters

Launched map tasks=2

Launched reduce tasks=1

Data-local map tasks=2

Total time spent by all maps in occupied slots (ms)=146137

Total time spent by all reduces in occupied slots (ms)=441

Total time spent by all map tasks (ms)=14613

Total time spent by all reduce tasks (ms)=44120

Total vcore-seconds taken by all map tasks=146137

Total vcore-seconds taken by all reduce tasks=44120

Total megabyte-seconds taken by all map tasks=149644288

Total megabyte-seconds taken by all reduce tasks=45178880

Map-Reduce Framework

Map input records=5

Map output records=5

Map output bytes=45

Map output materialized bytes=67

Input split bytes=208

Combine input records=5

Combine output records=5

Reduce input groups=5

Reduce shuffle bytes=6

Reduce input records=5

Reduce output records=5

Spilled Records=10

Shuffled Maps =2

Failed Shuffles=0

Merged Map outputs=2

GC time elapsed (ms)=948

CPU time spent (ms)=5160

Physical memory (bytes) snapshot=47749120

Virtual memory (bytes) snapshot=2899349504

Total committed heap usage (bytes)=277684224

File Output Format Counters

Bytes Written=40

Step 8

The following command is used to verify the resultant files in the output folder.

```
$HADOOP_HOME/bin/hadoop fs -ls output_dir/
```

Step 9

The following command is used to see the output in **Part-00000**file. This file is generated by HDFS.

```
$HADOOP_HOME/bin/hadoop fs -cat output_dir/part-00000
```

Below is the output generated by the MapReduce program.

```
1981   34
1984   40
1985   45
```

Step 10

The following command is used to copy the output folder from HDFS to the local file system for analyzing.

```
$HADOOP_HOME/bin/hadoop fs -cat output_dir/part-00000/bin/hadoop dfs g
```

Virtual Box

Oracle VM VirtualBox (formerly Sun VirtualBox, Sun xVM VirtualBox and Innotek VirtualBox) is a free and open-source hosted hypervisor for x86 computers currently being developed by Oracle Corporation. Developed initially by Innotek GmbH, it was acquired by Sun Microsystems in 2008 which was in turn acquired by Oracle in 2010.

VirtualBox may be installed on a number of host operating systems, including: Linux, macOS, Windows, Solaris, and OpenSolaris. There are also ports to FreeBSD[4] and Genode.

It supports the creation and management of guest virtual machines running versions and derivations of Windows, Linux, BSD, OS/2, Solaris, Haiku, OSx86 and others,and limited virtualization of macOS guests on Apple hardware.

For some guest operating systems, a "Guest Additions" package of device drivers and system applications is available which typically improves performance, especially that of graphics.

Installing VirtualBox

To start with, we will download VirtualBox and install it. We should follow the steps given below for the installation.

Step 1 – To download VirtualBox, click on the following link https://www.virtualbox.org/wiki/Downloads Now, depending on your OS, select which version to install. In our case, it will be the first one (Windows host).

Step 2 – Once the option is selected, click on "Next".

Step 3 – You have the option asking where to install the application. We can leave it as default and click on "Next".

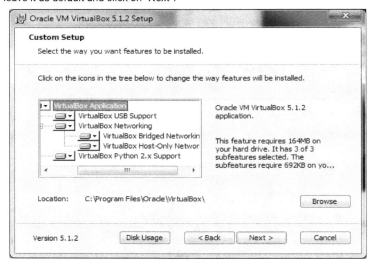

Step 4 – Once the options are selected as shown in the following screenshot, click on Next.

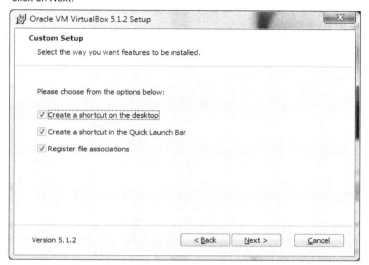

Step 5 – A dialog box will come up asking whether to proceed with the installation. Click "Yes".

Step 6 – In the next step, click on "Install".

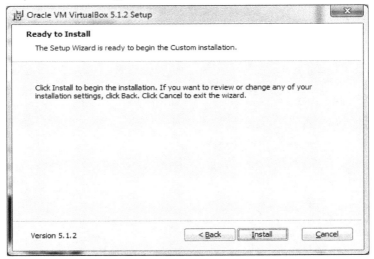

Step 7 – Tick the start VirtualBox check box and click on "Finish".

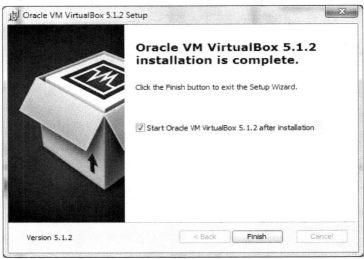

Step 8 – VirtualBox application will now open as shown in the following screenshot. Now, we are ready to install the virtual machines.

Creating a VM with VirtualBox

To create a virtual machine with Oracle VirtualBox, we should follow the steps given below.

Step 1 − To begin with, click on the "Oracle VM VirtualBox" icon on the desktop as shown in the screenshot below.

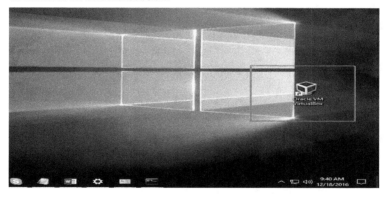

Step 2 − The next step is to click on "New" button, which is in the top left hand side of the screen.

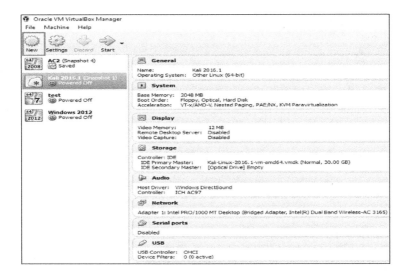

Step 3 – A table will pop-up requesting you the parameters for the virtual machine. These will be –

- **Name** – We have to put a friendly name for this Virtual Machine.

- **Type** – Enter the OS that is going to be installed on it.

- **Version** – Enter the specific version for that OS, which we have selected earlier.

Once all the above parameters are filled, click on "Next".

Step 4 – Select the amount of memory that you need to allocate in this VM →
Click on "Next".

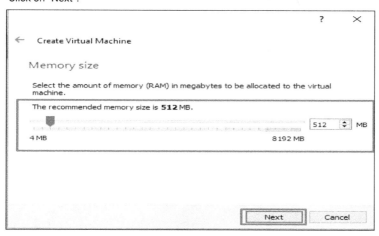

Step 5 – Check one of the three options for the HDD and click on "Create".

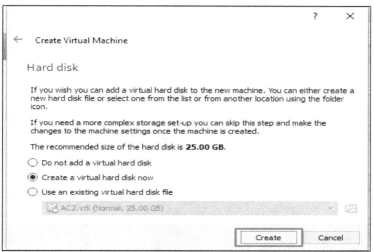

Step 6 – Select a file extension for your virtual HDD (It is recommended to use a common file extension that most of the hypervisors use like VHD) → click on "Next".

Step 7 – Choose whether you want the Virtual HDD as dynamic or fixed. This is based on your needs → Click on "Next".

Step 8 – Put a name for your virtual HDD file and select the disk size for your VM → Click on "Create".

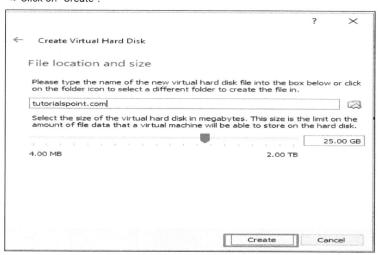

All the above steps can be done in one shot by selecting the "Expert mode".

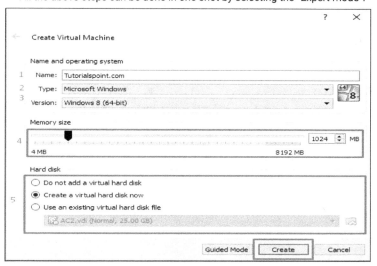

The virtual machine created will be as shown in the screenshot below.

Setting up Networking with VirtualBox

There are two types of networking modes in VirtualBox, which are –

- Nat Networks and
- Host-only Networks.

Both of these are explained in detail below.

Nat Networks

For setting up Nat Networks, we should follow the steps given below.

Step 1 – Go to Oracle VM VirtualBox Manager → Click on "Preferences…"

Step 2 – Click on "Network" and then on the left panel click on the "NAT Networks" tab.

Step 3 – Click on the "+" button, which is highlighted in the screenshot below.

Step 4 – Here, we have to put the "Network Name" and the IP range for this network that will be NAT-ed, in order to have access to internet and to other networks.

Host-only Networks

For setting up Host-only Networks, we should follow the steps given below.

Step 1 – If you click on the "Host-only Networks" tab, you can create networks that are isolated from the other networks. However, VM hosts communicate with each other and the Hypervisor machine. Click on the "+" sign.

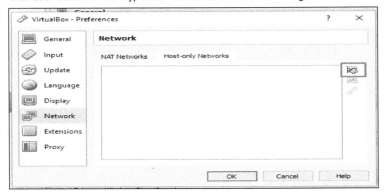

Step 2 – The host interface will continue to be created as shown in the screenshot below.

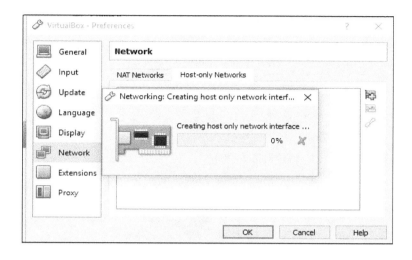

Step 3 − If you click on 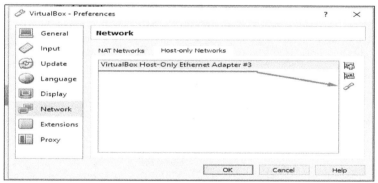 button, you can edit the settings.

Step 4 – If you want your host machines to take "DHCP IP", click on the "DHCP Server" tab and check the box "Enable Server" → Click "OK".

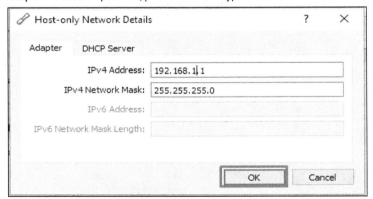

Step 5 – In the "Adapter" tab, put the IP of the hypervisor.

After all these preparations for setting up the network modes is complete. It is now time to assign a network to our VMs.

To do this, Click on the VMs on the left side of the panel, then right click on the "Network" option and a table will be open.

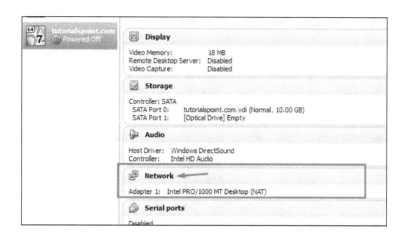

You can have up to four Ethernet adaptors per machine. The following image has four sections highlighted, which are explained below.

- Check the box "Enable Network Adapter" to enable the vNIC on the VM and attach it to one network.

- You can have many networks created, so we have to select one of them in the "Name" dropdown box.

- In the adapter type dropdown-box, we have to select a physical NIC that the hypervisor has.

- Promiscuous Mode: Here, we can select "Deny", if we do not want the VMs to communicate with each other.

Once all the above parameters are completed. Click on "OK".

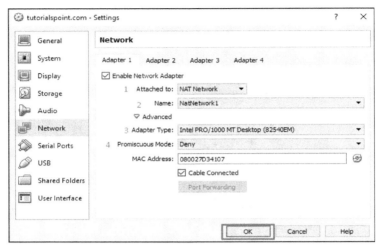

Allocating Processors & Memory to a VM

To allocate processors and memory to a virtual machine using VirtualBox, we should follow the steps given below.

Step 1 – To allocate a processor and memory, you have to click on "Settings" after you have selected the VM.

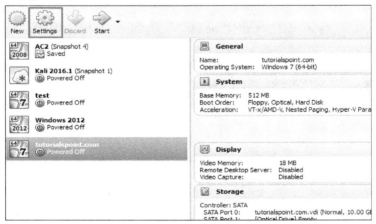

Step 2 – Click on "System" on the left side tab, then click on the "Motherboard" tab. Move the arrow left or right to allocate the memory as shown in the screenshot below.

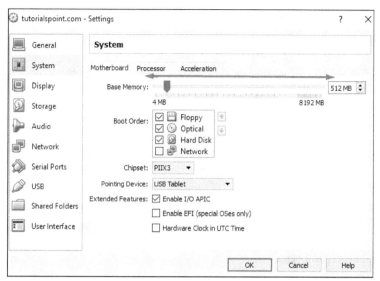

Step 3 – To allocate processors, click on the "Processor" tab. Move the arrow left or right to allocate the number of processors as shown in the screenshot below.

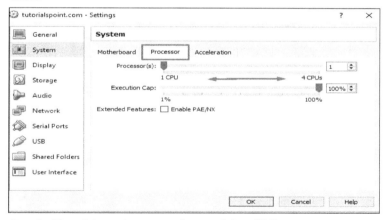

Step 4 – After all those changes are done → click on "OK".

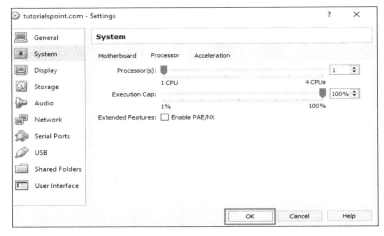

Duplicating a VM Using VirtualBox

To duplicate a virtual machine using VirtualBox, we should follow the steps given below.

Step 1 – To duplicate a VM that we created before, right click on the VM and select "Clone". A wizard will open.

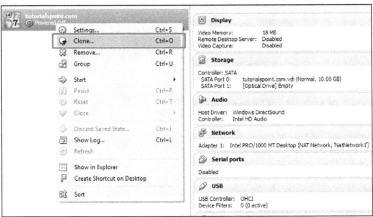

Step 2 – Write the name of the cloning machine and click on "Next".

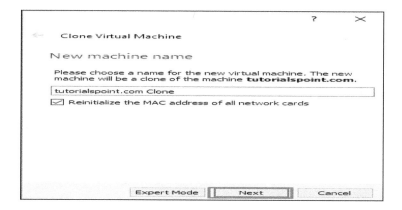

Step 3 − Select one of the options and Click on "Clone".

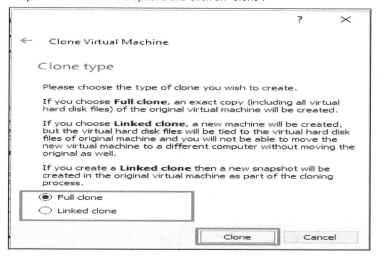

Step 4 − The newly created VM will be as shown in the following screenshot.

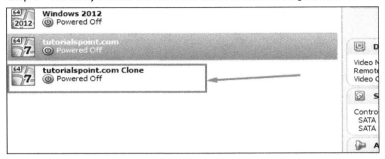

Deleting a VM on VirtualBox

To delete a virtual machine on VirtualBox, we should follow the steps given below.

Step 1 − To start with, we have to right click on the VM that we want to delete and then click on "Remove".

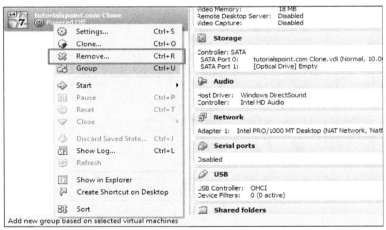

Step 2 − To delete a virtual machine completely, select "Delete all files".

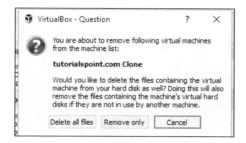

VirtualBox - Question

You are about to remove following virtual machines from the machine list:

tutorialspoint.com Clone

Would you like to delete the files containing the virtual machine from your hard disk as well? Doing this will also remove the files containing the machine's virtual hard disks if they are not in use by another machine.

Delete all files   Remove only   Cancel

Google App Engine

Google App Engine (often referred to as GAE or simply **App Engine**) is a web framework and **cloud computing** platform for developing and hosting web applications in **Google**-managed data centers. Applications are sandboxed and run across multiple servers.

App Engine Physical Deployment Diagram

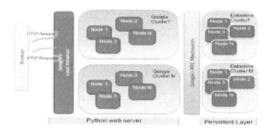

Getting Started: Setting Up Your Development Environment

Learn how to set up your build environment for app development and deployment to Google App Engine Standard. The supported Java development and build environments are IntelliJ IDEA, Eclipse, Apache Maven, and Gradle.

Install the Google Cloud SDK command-line tool.

Install and configure App Engine plugins for Eclipse, IntelliJ, Gradle, and Maven.

Create a new App Engine project.

Installing required SDKs

1. If you haven't already installed Java SE 8 SDK, install the Java SE 8 Development Kit (JDK).
2. Install the latest version of the Google Cloud SDK.

3. Install the App Engine Java component:

gcloud components install app-engine-java

4. Authorize your user account:

gcloud auth application-default login

5. Optionally, to create a service account run gcloud auth activate-service-account --key-file=your_key.json. For more information, see Authorizing Cloud SDK Tools.

Configuring your development environment

Before you begin:

1. Install Eclipse IDE for Java EE Developers, version 4.6 or later:
   DOWNLOAD ECLIPSE
2. If you have the Google Plugin for Eclipse installed, complete the migrating from GPE procedures.

Install the plugin:

1. Drag the install button into your running Eclipse workspace:

   Or from inside Eclipse, select **Help > Eclipse Marketplace...** and search for **Google Cloud**.
2. Restart Eclipse when prompted.

Creating a new App Engine project

1. Click the **Google Cloud Platform** toolbar button .
2. Select **Create New Project > Google App Engine Standard Java Project**.

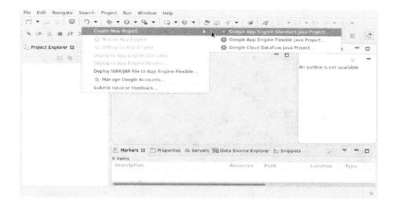

3. Enter a **Project name** and (optionally) a Java package.

4. To create a Maven-based App Engine project, check **Create as Maven Project** and enter a Maven **Group ID** and **Artifact ID**.
5. Select the libraries (App Engine API, Google Cloud Endpoints, and Objectify) to include in the project.
6. Click **Finish**.

The wizard generates a native Eclipse project, with a simple servlet, that you can run and deploy from the IDE.

Open Stack

OpenStack is a set of software tools for building and managing cloud computing platforms for public and private clouds. Backed by some of the biggest companies in software development and hosting, as well as thousands of individual community members, many think that OpenStack is the future of cloud computing. OpenStack is managed by the OpenStack Foundation, a non-profit that oversees both development and community-building around the project.

Introduction to OpenStack

OpenStack lets users deploy virtual machines and other instances that handle different tasks for managing a cloud environment on the fly. It makes horizontal scaling easy, which means that tasks that benefit from running concurrently can easily serve more or fewer users on the fly by just spinning up more instances. For example, a mobile application that needs to communicate with a remote server might be able to divide the work of communicating with each user across many different instances, all communicating with one another but scaling quickly and easily as the application gains more users.

And most importantly, OpenStack is open source software, which means that anyone who chooses to can access the source code, make any changes or modifications they need, and freely share these changes back out to the community at large. It also means that OpenStack has the benefit of thousands of developers all over the world working in tandem to develop the strongest, most robust, and most secure product that they can.

How is OpenStack used in a cloud environment?

The cloud is all about providing computing for end users in a remote environment, where the actual software runs as a service on reliable and scalable servers rather than on each end-user's computer. Cloud computing can refer to a lot of different things, but typically the industry talks about running different items "as a service"—software, platforms, and infrastructure. OpenStack falls into the latter category and is considered Infrastructure as a Service (IaaS). Providing infrastructure means that OpenStack makes it easy for users to quickly add new instance, upon which other cloud components can run. Typically, the infrastructure then runs a "platform" upon which a developer can create software applications that are delivered to the end users.

What are the components of OpenStack?

OpenStack is made up of many different moving parts. Because of its open nature, anyone can add additional components to OpenStack to help it to meet their needs. But the OpenStack community has collaboratively identified nine key components that are a part of the "core" of OpenStack, which are distributed as a part of any OpenStack system and officially maintained by the OpenStack community.

• **Nova** is the primary computing engine behind OpenStack. It is used for deploying and managing large numbers of virtual machines and other instances to handle computing tasks.

• **Swift** is a storage system for objects and files. Rather than the traditional idea of a referring to files by their location on a disk drive, developers can instead refer to a unique identifier referring to the file or piece of information and let OpenStack decide where to store this information. This makes scaling easy, as developers don't have the worry about the capacity on a single system behind the software. It also allows the system, rather than the developer, to worry about how best to make sure that data is backed up in case of the failure of a machine or network connection.

• **Cinder** is a block storage component, which is more analogous to the traditional notion of a computer being able to access specific locations on a disk drive. This more traditional way of accessing files might be important in scenarios in which data access speed is the most important consideration.

• **Neutron** provides the networking capability for OpenStack. It helps to ensure that each of the components of an OpenStack deployment can communicate with one another quickly and efficiently.

• **Horizon** is the dashboard behind OpenStack. It is the only graphical interface to OpenStack, so for users wanting to give OpenStack a try, this may be the first component they actually "see." Developers can access all of the components of OpenStack individually through an application programming interface (API), but the dashboard provides system administrators a look at what is going on in the cloud, and to manage it as needed.

• **Keystone** provides identity services for OpenStack. It is essentially a central list of all of the users of the OpenStack cloud, mapped against all of the services provided by the cloud, which they have permission to use. It provides multiple means of access, meaning developers can easily map their existing user access methods against Keystone.

• **Glance** provides image services to OpenStack. In this case, "images" refers to images (or virtual copies) of hard disks. Glance allows these images to be used as templates when deploying new virtual machine instances.

- **Ceilometer** provides telemetry services, which allow the cloud to provide billing services to individual users of the cloud. It also keeps a verifiable count of each user's system usage of each of the various components of an OpenStack cloud. Think metering and usage reporting.

- **Heat** is the orchestration component of OpenStack, which allows developers to store the requirements of a cloud application in a file that defines what resources are necessary for that application. In this way, it helps to manage the infrastructure needed for a cloud service to run.

Who is OpenStack for?

You may be an OpenStack user right now and not even know it. As more and more companies begin to adopt OpenStack as a part of their cloud toolkit, the universe of applications running on an OpenStack backend is ever-expanding.

How do I get started with OpenStack?

If you just want to give OpenStack a try, one good resource for spinning the wheels without committing any physical resources is TryStack. TryStack lets you test your applications in a sandbox environment to better understand how OpenStack works and whether it is the right solution for you.

Ready to learn more? Every month, we publish a collection of the best new guides, tips, tricks, tutorials for OpenStack.

OpenStack is always looking for new contributors. Consider joining the OpenStack Foundation or reading this introduction to getting started with contributing to OpenStack.

Cloud Federation

Cloud Federation refers to the unionization of software, infrastructure and platform services from disparate networks that can be accessed by a client via the internet. The federation of cloud resources is facilitated through network gateways that connect public or external clouds, private or internal clouds (owned by a single entity) and/or community clouds (owned by several cooperating entities); creating a hybrid cloud computing environment. It is important to note that federated cloud computing services still rely on the existence of physical data centers.

From Cisco's Cloud Computing Primer: "One definition of cloud federation as proposed by Reuven Cohen of Enomaly follows: Cloud federation manages consistency and access controls when two or more independent geographically distributed clouds share either authentication, files, computing resources, command and control, or access to storage resources." [More like it, and more detailed ... but still not quite there.]

The establishment of a federation between two generic systems A and B will typically mean that resources and functionality hosted by one system is made available to the other. In a symmetrical relationship, the authorities respectively controlling A and B would share equally, and when everything is shared so that A is controllable completely from B and B from A, it's hard not to think of them as having merged – except for the fact that it only takes a change of policy by one authority to end the arrangement. With federated clouds, however, the relationship is typically asymmetric; the enterprise will generally want to use the facilities provided by a Cloud Service Provider (CSP), rather than the converse. However, asymmetric does not mean one-way: the right information must flow in each direction for the management of a cloud federation to work.

In a cloud federation, the boundary between clouds is still there, but aspects of the boundary that would normally prevent interoperability will have been overcome. Whether or not the boundary is apparent will depend on who you are and what you are trying to accomplish. If you are an end-user trying to access a desktop hosted on a remote cloud, then every effort will have been taken to hide this boundary from you, so that you are in a state of blissful ignorance (at least, with respect to the federation). If you are an administrator trying to balance resource usage across your datacentre's private cloud and a third-party public cloud (perhaps to minimise cost), then you very much want to be able to see the boundary and what's happening either side of it. So the important point is not that the federation boundary is hidden, but that it can be hidden when you need it to be.

In order to achieve federation, two issues must be overcome: mutual mistrust, and technical discontinuity. Mutual mistrust can be mitigated by a robust approach to security, both within the cooperating clouds and across them, but this can only raise confidence so far: other measures (such as CSP certification and SLAs) must be employed to finish the job. The last resort will always be litigation (i.e. deferring to a higher authority for issue resolution). In any case, the acceptability question to be answered is not "is this federation secure?" but "is it secure enough, in the right ways, for what I want to do?" Do bear in mind, also, that ensuring security within each cloud is not sufficient to ensure security between clouds – this needs approaching as an issue in its own right, and any inter-cloud and infra-cloud security mechanisms must also interwork where needed. *Hic dracones:* as Alexander Pope might have said, never was a little learning a more dangerous thing than in the field of distributed security. Mutual mistrust will probably also exist in other areas, creating judicial, contractual, economic, social, political and cultural boundaries, all of which may need attention, discussion, and eventual agreement in ways to overcome them.

CLOUD FEDERATION BENEFITS

The federation of cloud resources allows clients to optimize enterprise IT service delivery. The federation of cloud resources allows a client to choose the best cloud services provider, in terms of flexibility, cost and availability of services, to meet a particular business or technological need within their organization.

Federation across different cloud resource pools allows applications to run in the most appropriate infrastructure environments. The federation of cloud resources also allows an enterprise to distribute workloads around the globe, move data between disparate networks and implement innovative security models for user access to cloud resources.

CLOUD FEDERATION IMPLEMENTATION

One weakness that exists in the federation of cloud resources is the difficulty in brokering connectivity between a client and a given external cloud provider, as they each possess their own unique network addressing scheme. To resolve this issue, cloud providers must grant clients the permission to specify an addressing scheme for each server the cloud provider has extended to the internet. This provides customers with the ability to access cloud services without the need for reconfiguration when using resources from different service providers. Cloud federation can also be implemented behind a firewall, providing clients with a menu of cloud services provided by one or more trusted entities.

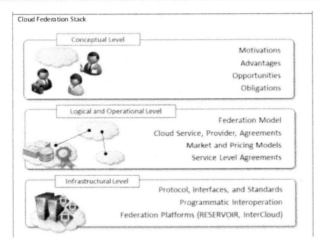

A layered model of Cloud services

The top layer is the software layer, which deals with requirements in executing the application within the context of the key performance metrics (KPM) of the application offering in addition to application execution environment. For WRF this exemplary KPM is completion time for a weather forecast of a user specified geographic region with a certain resolution. The application service layer is aware of the KPMs and software and how they translate into resources at the PaaS. The information for this mapping from KPM at SaaS to PaaS resources is developed through off line experiments and input from online results.

The next layer in the stack corresponds to the Platform as a Service layer. This is traditionally the most overloaded term in the Cloud. Specifically, we define the intrinsic characteristics of a PaaS provider in this chapter:

Development library. A PaaS offering allows a developer to build the target application by using a defined library.

Runtime environment. The platform has a runtime component that manages the application's underlying aspects.

Layer decoupling. It is decoupled from the upper and lower layers. This means that, first, the platform layer does not have any knowledge of the application specific details. Second, it is agnostic to the underlying infrastructure.

Elasticity and Fault tolerance. Finally, the platform layer needs to support operations that will result in the Cloud's elastic behavior. This means that it needs to allow scalable resource allocation and have mechanisms to deal with failures.

The PaaS layer corresponds to the traditional concept of middleware and represents the bridge between application requirements and elastic infrastructure resource management. This layer does not consider the actual infrastructure – *e.g.*, how many Virtual Machines need to be provisioned –, but rather a higher representation of execution units such as tasks, processes, threads, *etc.*

Well-known examples of PaaS offerings in the Cloud are Google App Engine and Microsoft Azure. However, this layer can be implemented by different means. An example of this in the WRF application stack would be MPI [6]. MPI is both a development library and a runtime environment, it does not consider either application specific details nor make assump-tions about the underlying resources, can be executed for a varying number of processes, and offers a simple fault tolerant behavior (by terminating a job when one of the processes fails). The newer specification of MPI-2 includes further fea-tures to dynamically add and remove MPI tasks to/from running applications and thus would be useful in exploiting the elasticity capability of Cloud resources.

Finally, the IaaS layer represents the resources of infrastructures on top of which the rest of the stack is supported. The concepts managed at the IaaS layer correspond to Virtual Machines, disk images, network connectivity and number of processors, for example.

## 7

Cloud Computing Trends

This section fills in some of the details, asks some deeper questions, looks at current trends, such as the shift to mobile devices, and explores challenging issues like privacy and security.

Growth

The figures speak for themselves: in every IT survey, news report, and pundit's op-ed, cloud computing seems the only show in town. Back in 2008, almost a decade ago, the Pew Internet project reported that 69 percent of all Internet users had "either stored data online or used a web-based software application" (in other words, by their definition, used some form of cloud computing). In 2009, Gartner priced the value of cloud computing at $58.6 billion, in 2010 at $68.3 billion, in 2012 at over $102 billion, and in 2017 at $260 billion. In 2013, management consultants McKinsey and Company forecast cloud computing (and related trends like big data, growing mobilization, and the Internet of Things) could have a "collective economic impact" of between $10–20 trillion by 2025. In 2016, Amazon revealed that its AWS offshoot, the world's biggest provider of cloud computing, is now a $10 billion-a-year business; the Microsoft Cloud isn't far behind.

A matter of definitions

So the numbers keep on creeping up and it's an exciting trend, to be sure. But there's one important word of caution: how you measure and forecast something as vague as "the cloud" depends on how you define it: if the definition keeps expanding, perhaps that's one reason why the market keeps expanding too? Way back in the 1990s, no-one described Yahoo! Mail or Hotmail as examples of cloud computing, Geocities was simply a community of amateur websites, and Amazon and eBay were just new ways of finding and buying old stuff. In 2010, in its breathless eagerness to talk up cloud computing, the Pew Internet project had rounded up every web-based service and application it could think of and fired it to the sky. Wordpress and Twitter were examples of cloud blogging, Google Docs and Gmail were cloud-based, and suddenly so too were Yahoo! Mail, buying things from eBay and Amazon, and even (bizarrely) RSS feeds (which date back to the late 1990s). Using "the cloud" as a loose synonym for "the Web," then expressing astonishment that it's growing so fast seems tautologous at best, since we know the Internet and Web have grown simply by virtue of having more connected users and more (especially more mobile) devices. According to Pew, what these users prized were things like easy access to services from absolutely anywhere and simple data storing or sharing. This is a circular argument as well: one reason we like "the cloud" is because we've defined it as a bunch of likeable websites—Facebook, Twitter, Gmail, and all the rest.

Business benefits

Businesses have shrewder and more interesting reasons for liking the cloud. Instead of depending on Microsoft Office, to give one very concrete example, they can use free, cloud-based open-source alternatives such as Google Docs. So there are obvious cost and practical advantages: you don't have to worry about expensive software licenses or security updates, and your staff can simply and securely share documents across business locations (and work on them just as easily from home). Using cloud computing to run applications has a similarly compelling business case: you can buy in as much (or little) computing resource as you need at any given moment, so there's no problem of having to fund expensive infrastructure upfront. If you run something like an ecommerce website on cloud hosting, you can scale it up or down for the holiday season or the sales, just as you need to. Best of all, you don't need a geeky IT department because—beyond commodity computers running open-source web browsers—you don't need IT.

Spot the difference

When we say cloud computing is growing, do we simply mean that more people (and more businesses) are using the Web (and using it to do more) than they used to? Actually we do—and that's why it's important not to be too loose with our definitions. Cloud web hosting is much more sophisticated than ordinary web-hosting, for example, even though—from the viewpoint of the webmaster and the person accessing a website—both work in almost exactly the same way. This web page is coming to you courtesy of cloud hosting where, a decade ago, it ran on a simple, standalone server. It's running on the same open-source Apache server software that it used then and you can access it in exactly the same way (with http and html). The difference is that it can cope with a suddenly spike in traffic in the way it couldn't back then: if everyone in the United States accessed this web page at the same time, the grid of servers hosting it would simply scale and manage the demand intelligently. The photos and graphics on the page (and some of the other technical stuff that happens behind the scenes) are served from a cloud-based **Content Delivery Network (CDN)**: each file comes from a server in Washington, DC, Singapore, London, or Mumbai, or a bunch of other "edge locations," depending on where in the world you (the browser) happen to be.

This example illustrates three key points of difference between cloud-based services and applications and similar ones accessed over the web. One is the concept of **elasticity** (which is a similar idea to **scalability**): a cloud service or application isn't limited to what a particular server can cope with; it can automatically expand or contract its capacity as needed. Another is the **dynamic** nature of cloud services: they're not provided from a single, static server. A third, related idea is that cloud services are **seamless**—whether you're a developer or an end user, everything looks the same, however, wherever, and with whatever device you use it.

Elastic and scalable: Liquid Web's Storm on Demand allows you to set up a cloud server in a matter of minutes. With a couple of mouse clicks, you can resize your server (upgrade or downgrade the memory, for example) to cope with changes in demand—for example, in the run up to a Black Friday sale. Every aspect of the service is pay-as-you-go. It's easy to use even if you have little or no experience of setting up or managing dedicated servers.

Mobilization

One of the biggest single drivers of cloud computing is the huge shift away from desktop computers to mobile devices, which (historically, at least) had much less processing power onboard. Web-connected smartphones, tablets, Kindles, and other mobile devices are examples of what used to be called "thin clients" or "network computers" because they rely on the servers they're connected to, via the network (usually the Internet), to do most of the work. A related trend referred to as **bring your own device (BYOD)** reflects the way that many companies now allow their employees to logon to corporate networks or websites using their own laptops, tablets, and smartphones.

From the smartphone in your pocket to the mythical fridge that orders your milk, the number and range of devices connected to the Internet is increasing all the time. A new trend called the Internet of Things anticipates a massive increase in connected devices as everyday objects and things with built-in sensors (home heating controllers, home security webcams, and even parcels in transit) get their own IP addresses and become capable of sending and receiving data to anything or anyone else that's online. That will fuel the demand for cloud computing even more.

The shift to mobile devices and the growth of cloud computing are mutually reinforcing trends. Mobile devices are much more useful thanks to cloud-based apps like these, provided by Google. In other words, one reason for buying a mobile is because of the extra (cloud-based) things you can do with it. But these services are also thriving because they have ever-increasing numbers of users, many of them on smartphones.

How significant is the shift to mobile? By any measurement, phenomenal and dramatic. Bearing in mind that there was only one functioning mobile phone in 1973 when Martin Cooper made the first cellphone call, it's staggering to find that there are now an estimated 8 billion mobile subscriptions (more than one for every person on the planet). By 2012, Goldman Sachs was telling us that 66 percent of Net-connected devices were mobiles, compared to just 29 percent desktops. Mobile Internet traffic finally overtook desktop traffic in 2014/15, according to Comscore and, in response, Google rolled out a "mobile-friendly" algorithm in 2015 to encourage webmasters to optimize their sites so they worked equally well on smartphones. In 2018, Google began indexing the smartphone versions of websites in preference to the desktop versions with its new, so-called mobile-first index.

Cloud computing makes it possible for cellphones to be smartphones and for tablets to do the sorts of things that we used to do on desktops, but it also encourages us to do more things with those devices—and so on, in a virtuous circle. For example, if you buy a smartphone, you don't simply do things on your phone that you used to do on your PC: you spend more time online overall, using apps and services that you previously wouldn't have used at all. Cloud computing made mobile devices feasible, so people bought them in large numbers, driving the development of more mobile apps and better mobile devices, and so on.

More types of cloud

Stare high to the sky and you can watch clouds drift by or, if you're more scientific and nuanced, start to tease out the differences between cumulus, cirrus, and stratus. In much the same way, computing aficionados draw a distinction between different types of cloud. **Public clouds** are provided by people such as Amazon, Google, and IBM: in theory, all users share space and time on the same cloud and access it the same way. Many companies, for example, use Gmail to power their Internet mail and share documents using Google Drive—in pretty much the same way that you or I might do so as individuals. **Private clouds** work technically the same way but service a single company and are either managed exclusively by that company or by one of the big cloud providers on their behalf. They're fully integrated with the company's existing networks, Intranet, databases, and infrastructure, and span countries or continents in much the same way. Increasingly, companies find neither of these bald alternatives quite fits the bill—they need elements of each—so they opt for **hybrid clouds** that combine the best of both worlds, hooking up their existing IT infrastructure to a public cloud system provided by someone like Amazon or Google. Other trends to watch include the development of **personal clouds**, where you configure your own home network to work like a mini-cloud (so, for example, all your mobile devices can store and access files seamlessly), and **peer-to-peer cloud computing**, in which the dynamic, scalable power of a cloud computing system is provided not by giant data centers but by many individual, geographically dispersed computers arriving on the network, temporarily contributing to it, and then leaving again (as already happens with collaborative science projects like SETI@home and ClimatePrediction.net).

Cloud concerns?

Security has always been an obvious concern for people who use cloud computing: if your data is remote and traveling back and forth over the Internet, what's to keep it safe? Perhaps surprisingly, many IT professionals think cloud-based systems are actually *more secure* than conventional ones. If you're buying into Google's, Amazon's, or Microsoft's cloud-based services, you're also buying into world-class expertise at keeping data safe; could you—or your IT team—manage security as well? Security can therefore be seen as a compelling reason to migrate to cloud-based systems rather than a reason to avoid them.

Privacy is a more nuanced and complex issue. While we all understand what we mean by keeping data secure, what do we mean by keeping it private in a world where users of cloud-based services like Twitter, Instagram, and Snapchat happily share anything and everything online? One of the complications is so-called **big data**, the statistical ("analytic") information that companies like Google and Facebook gather about the way we use their cloud-based services (and other websites that use those services). Google, for example, collects huge amounts of data through its advertising platforms and no-one knows exactly what happens to it afterward. Facebook knows an enormous amount about what people say they "like," which means it can compile detailed profiles of all its users. And Twitter knows what you tweet, retweet, and favorite—so it has similar data to Facebook. The quid-pro-quo for "free" web-based services and apps is that you pay for what you use with a loss of privacy, typically to power targeted advertisements.

Another complication is that privacy means different things in different parts of the world. In Europe, for example, the European Union has strict restrictions on how data can be moved in bulk from one country to another or shared by companies like Google that have multiple subsidiaries operating across countries and continents. While Internet-based cloud computing makes national boundaries obsolete, real-world laws still operate according to old-fashioned geography—and that could act as a serious brake on the aspirations of many big cloud providers.

No such thing as a free cloud?

When it comes to the everyday web services we all enjoy, there may be different kinds of clouds on the horizon. As web-based advertising dwindles in effectiveness, one future concern must be how companies like Google, Facebook, and Twitter will continue to fund their ever-growing, (essentially) cloud-based, services without using our data in increasingly dubious ways. Part of the reason for the huge growth in popularity of services like this is simply that they're free. Would Facebook be so popular if we had to pay for it through a monthly subscription? If Google Docs cost money, would we slink back to our desktop PCs and Microsoft Word? Can advertising continue to sustain an ever-growing field of cloud-based services and apps as the number of Internet users and Net-connected devices continues to grow? Watch this space!

Is cloud computing really better for the environment?

n theory, cloud computing is environmentally friendly because it uses fewer resources (servers, cooling systems, and all the rest) and less energy if 10 people share an efficiently run, centralized, cloud-based system than if each of them run their own inefficient local system. One hosting provider in the UK told me that his company has embraced cloud systems because it means they can handle more customers on far fewer physical servers, with big savings in equipment, maintenance, and energy costs. In theory, cloud computing should be a big win for the environment; in practice, it's not quite so simple.

Ironically, given the way we've defined cloud computing, it matters where your cloud servers are located and how they're powered. If they're in data centers powered by coal, instead of cleaner fuels such as natural gas or (better still) renewable energy, the overall environmental impact could be worse than your current setup. There's been a lot of debate about the energy use of huge data centers, partly thanks to Greenpeace highlighting the issue once a year since 2009. In its 2011 report, it ranked cloud computing providers like Akamai and Amazon on eco-friendliness, alongside companies like Facebook, Google, and Twitter whose services are underpinned by a massive global network of data centers. By 2017, in a report called Clicking Clean, Greenpeace was congratulating around 20 of the biggest data center operators (including Apple, Facebook, and Google) for starting on the path toward 100 percent renewable energy. In the United States in particular, quite a few cloud (and web hosting) providers explicitly state whether their servers are powered by conventional or green energy, and it's relatively easy to find carbon-neutral service providers if that's an important factor for your business and its CSR (corporate social responsibility) objectives.

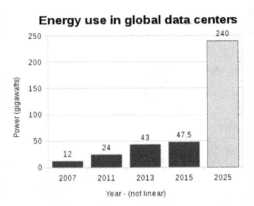

Energy use in global data centers

Growth in energy use in data centers from 2007 onward. Drawn by us using data from the 2012 study by DatacenterDynamics (DCD) Intelligence published in Computer Weekly, October 8, 2012; 2015 data from Data Centers 'Going Green' To Reduce A Carbon Footprint Larger Than The Airline Industry"; 2025 projection from 'Tsunami of data' could consume one fifth of global electricity by 2025: The Guardian, 11 December 2017.

When it comes to overall impact on the planet, there's another issue to consider. If cloud services simply move things you would do in your own office or home to the cloud, that's one thing; the environmental impact merely transfers elsewhere. But a lot of cloud- and Internet-based services are encouraging us to use more computers and gadgets like iPads and iPhones for longer, spending more time online, and doing more things that we didn't previously do at all. In that sense, cloud computing is helping to increase global energy use and greenhouse gas emissions —so describing it as environmentally friendly is highly misleading.

That was evident from a 2012 study by DatacenterDynamics (DCD) Intelligence, the British Computer Society, and partners (reported in Computer Weekly), which showed that global energy use from data centers grew from 12 gigawatts (GW) in 2007 to 24GW in 2011 and predicted it would reach 43GW some time in 2013. However, a follow-up study revealed a significant slowing down of the rate of growth in cloud power consumption, from 19 percent in 2011/2 to around 7 percent in 2013. Growing concerns about the impact of cloud computing have also prompted imaginative new solutions. Later in 2013, for example, researchers at Trinity College Dublin and IBM announced they'd found a way to reduce cloud emissions by over 20 percent by using smart load-balancing algorithms to spread out data processing between different data centers. In April 2018, Google announced that it had successfully offset all its conventional electricity use through matched investments in renewable (wind and solar) energy.

Even so, with cloud computing predicted to become a $5 trillion business by 2020, global power consumption seems certain to go on increasing. Ultimately, the global environment, the bottomline trend—ever-increasing energy consumption—is the one that matters. It's no good congratulating yourself on switching to diet Cola if you're drinking four times more of it than you used to. In 2016, Peter Judge of DatacenterDynamics summed things up pithily: "No one talks much about total energy used by data centers because the figures you get for that are annoying, depressing and frustrating.... The truth is: data center power is out of control."

From Google searches to Facebook updates and super-convenient Hotmail, most of us value the benefits of cloud computing very highly, so the energy consumption of data centers is bound to increase—and ensuring those big, power-hungry servers are fueled by green energy will become increasingly important in the years to come.

## 8

Case-Study of Cloud Computing

Royal Mail

> **Subject of Case-Study:**Using Cloud Computing for effective communication among staff.

> **Reason for using Cloud Computing:**Reducing the cost made after communication for 28,000 employees and to provide advance features and interface of e-mail services to their employees.

Royal mail group, a postal service in U.K, is the only government organization in U.K that serves over 24 million customers through its 12000 post offices and 3000 separate processing sites. Its logistics systems and parcel-force worldwide handles around 404 million parcel a year. And to do this they need an effective communicative medium. They have recognized the advantage of Cloud Computing and implemented it to their system. It has shown an outstanding performance in inter-communication.

Before moving on to Cloud system, the organization was struggling with the out-of-date software, and due to which the operational efficiency was getting compromised. As soon as the organization switched on to Cloud System, 28000 employees were supplied with their new collaboration suite, giving them access to tools such as instant messaging and presence awareness. The employees got more storage place than on local server. The employees became much more productive.

Looking to the success of Cloud Computing in e-mail services and communication .The second strategic move of Royal Mail Group, was to migrating from physical servers to virtual servers, upto 400 servers to create a private cloud based on Microsoft hyper V. This would give a fresh look and additional space to their employees desktop and also provides latest modern exchange environment.

The hyper V project by RMG's (Royal Mail Group) is estimated to save around 1.8 million pound for them in future and will increase the efficiency of the organization's internal IT system.

While using cloud computing, the major issue that concerns the users is about its security.

One concern is that cloud providers themselves may have access to customer's unencrypted data- whether it's on disk, in memory or transmitted over the network.